Galloway's 5K/10K Running

GALLOWAY'S
Running
5K/10K

TRAINING FOR RUNNERS AND WALKERS

Jeff Galloway

Meyer & Meyer Sport

British Library Cataloguing in Publication Data

A catalogue record for this book is available from the British Library

Galloway's 5K/10K Running

Maidenhead: Meyer & Meyer Sport (UK) Ltd., 2021

ISBN: 978-1-78255-206-2

© 2021 by Meyer & Meyer Sport (UK) Ltd.
4th Edition of the 1st Edition 2008

Aachen, Auckland, Beirut, Cairo, Cape Town, Dubai, Hägendorf, Hong Kong, Indianapolis, Maidenhead, Manila, New Delhi, Singapore, Sydney, Tehran, Vienna

 Member of the World Sport Publishers' Association (WSPA)

Printed by: Print Consult GmbH, Munich, Germany

ISBN: 978-1-78255-206-2
Email: info@m-m-sports.com
www.m-m-sports.com

Contents

Chapter 1

5K-10K: THE MOST POPULAR DISTANCES

- Runners and walkers are enrolling in 5Ks and 10Ks in record numbers

- This book is designed to support runners and walkers in 5K and 10K events, with information for faster times, if desired

- Beginners can identify with a 3- to 6-mile goal

- The training does not have to interrupt a busy lifestyle

- Experienced runners use these distances as speed tests for longer events

- The 5K and 10K races are usually easy to find in most communities

- Those who have a plan for training and racing, have a better time (finish sooner and have more fun)

Gathering together before and during a road race brings us back to our roots. Experts explain that before ancient man developed tools, survival was based upon distance running and walking. Through continual migrations (thousands of foot-miles a year) our ancestors gathered food and escaped predators. Millions of years of adapting to these long treks produced muscles, tendons, bones, energy systems, and cardiovascular capacity to cover extremely long distances. A series of psychological rewards also developed, which we enjoy today when we run and walk at the correct pace for a prolonged distance.

Just as the primary goal of the ancient migration was to reach the destination, finishing your first 5K or 10K brings an unexpected sense of satisfaction and accomplishment. Since many local charities use these distances to raise funds, you get three major reward systems during one event: The satisfaction of improving fitness, achieving a goal, while helping a non-profit organization in your community.

As beginners push back their physical barriers, they often learn more about their physical and psychological capabilities than in other life experiences. The simple "to finish" program in this book has an almost zero failure rate when done in supervised programs. But even beginners have days when the ego pushes them beyond current performance capabilities. On these workouts, most are surprised to find much more inner strength than expected. But even when mistakes are made during a 5K/10K program, the consequences are usually easy to repair, as valuable lessons are learned.

Veterans will find in this book a series of highly successful training programs, based upon time goals. You'll be introduced to various training components that will make the journey more interesting. Be careful if you're a veteran doing speed workouts: most of the injuries occur during these sessions. It is always best to be conservative.

Inside, you'll find a series of ways to enjoy walks, slow runs and faster workouts. As you overcome challenges, you'll expand your capacity to deal with other challenges in life. Endurance training blends body, mind and spirit into a team, producing a unique sense of achievement, with a positive attitude.

This book offers a series of tools which can give you control over your fitness, your attitude, your endurance, your fatigue, your aches/pains, and your vitality. By using the system that pulls them together, you become the captain of an injury-free ship—steering toward positive experiences.

The information in this book is passed from one runner to another. The advice comes from more than 50 years of running, and having been the "coach" to more than 500,000 runners through my e-coaching, running schools, retreats, books, and individual consultations. None of the suggestions inside are offered as medical advice. To get help in this area, see a doctor or appropriate medical expert.

I salute all who put themselves to a realistic challenge. If you haven't done this before, you have one of life's great rewards waiting for you; you have much more strength inside than you envisioned.

Chapter 2

SETTING GOALS AND PRIORITIES

By focusing on a few key elements, you have the opportunity to take control over the enjoyment of the endurance experience. If you're preparing for your first 5K or 10K event, I recommend that you choose the "to finish" schedule, and run/walk slower on every exercise session than you could go on that day. Be sure to read carefully the "run-walk-run" chapter. This method will lower the chance of aches, pains, and injuries.

Success on your first race is very important—and everyone can be successful. Even after the 20th or 100th race, you're more likely to remember the details of your first one. Your mission, therefore, should be to weave the training sessions and the race itself, to produce a series of good memories. The three behaviors will increase motivation for future training and racing.

TOP 3 GOALS FOR FIRST TIME 5K/10K RUNNERS

1. Finish in the upright position

2. Have a smile on your face

3. Want to do it again

RUNNING ENJOYMENT

Find a way to enjoy parts of every run/walk—even the speed training (if you are a time goal runner). Most of your runs/walks should be....mostly enjoyable. Insert a few social/scenic/mentally refreshing workouts. Your desire to exercise will be enhanced by scheduling these fun sessions first—at least one every week.

STAYING INJURY FREE

When injured runners review their journal, they often discover the causes of aches and pains. Make a list of past problems, and repeated challenges. After reading the injury section of this book, make the needed adjustments. Most runners I've worked with have found that the conservative training program adjustments in this book will reduce the "down days" to almost nothing.

AVOIDING OVERUSE OR BURNOUT

All of us receive the warning signs of overtraining. Unfortunately, we often ignore these or don't know what they are. Your training journal can track the aches, pains, loss of desire, unusual fatigue that lingers, etc. Spending a few minutes a day with your journal can help you gain control over your exercise future.

BECOMING THE CAPTAIN OF YOUR SHIP

When you balance stress and rest, endurance exercise bestows a sense of satisfaction and achievement that is unsurpassed. Intuitively, we know that this is good for us, mentally and physically. When we decide to use the monitoring tools in this book we take a major amount of control over fatigue, injuries, energy level, and enjoyment of physical activity.

WHEN TO SET A TIME GOAL

Wait until you have run at least one race before you attempt a time goal. I strongly recommend that veteran runners say well within their capabilities on their first attempt at each distance. Once the first one has been finished there is an interesting world of challenges in training for a time goal. Many veterans (myself included) decide to stay within current capabilities, using the "to finish" schedule to prepare for most races. This increases the chance that every race will be a positive experience.

I commend each person who decides to take on an endurance challenge. Almost everyone who makes it to the finish line will tap into a mysterious and complex source of inner strength: the human spirit. Enjoy the journey!

Chapter 3

IMPORTANT HEALTH INFORMATION

MEDICAL CHECK

Check with your doctor's office before you start a strenuous training program. Keep the doctor informed of cardiovascular system irregularities, other health warning signs, or aches and pains that could be injuries. At first, just tell your physician or head nurse how much running/walking you plan to be doing over the next year. Almost every person will be given the green light. If your doctor recommends against your plans, ask why.

Since there are so few people who cannot train even for strenuous goals (if they use a liberal run-walk-run formula), I suggest that you get a second opinion if your doctor tells you not to walk or run. Many health experts have said that if exercise were a medication, it would be the most heavily prescribed in history. The best medical advisor is one who wants you to get the type of physical activity that engages you—unless there are significant reasons not to do so.

Note: The information in this book is offered as advice from one runner to another, and is not meant to be medical advice. Having a doctor/advisor will not only help you through some problems more quickly, but contact with a responsive and supportive medical advisor will improve confidence and motivation, while reducing anxiety.

RISKS:
HEART DISEASE, LUNG INFECTIONS, SPEEDWORK INJURIES

Running tends to bestow a protective effect from cardiovascular disease. But more runners die of heart disease than any other cause, and are susceptible to the same risk factors as sedentary people. Like most other citizens, runners at risk usually don't know that they are. Runners and walkers can significantly reduce the chance of an incident by submitting to a few tests and taking appropriate action.

This short section is offered as a guide to help you take charge over your cardiovascular health to maintain a high level of fitness in the most important organ for longevity, and quality of life. As always, you need to get advice about your individual situation from a doctor who knows you, is familiar with the effects of exercise and the cardiovascular system.

Risk Factors

Get checked if you have two of these—or one that is serious

- Family history
- Poor lifestyle habits earlier in life (alcohol, drugs, poor diet, etc.)
- High fat/high cholesterol diet
- Have smoked—or still smoke
- Obese or severely overweight
- High blood pressure
- High cholesterol

Tests

- Stress test—heart is monitored during a run/strenuous walk which gradually increases in difficulty

- Cholesterol

- C reactive protein—has been an indicator of increased risk

- Heart scan—an electronic scan of the heart which shows calcification, and possible narrowing of arteries

- Radioactive dye test—very effective in locating specific blockages. Talk to your doctor about this.

- Carotid ultrasound test—helps to tell if you're at risk for stroke

- Ankle-brachial test—can detect plaque buildup in arteries throughout the body

None of these are foolproof. But by working with your cardiologist, you can increase your chance of living until the muscles just won't propel you further down the road—maybe beyond the age of 100.

SHOULD I RUN WHEN I HAVE A COLD?

There are so many individual health issues with a cold that you must talk with a doctor before you exercise when you have an infection. You will usually be given clearance over

the phone.

Lung infection—don't run! A virus in the lungs can move into the heart and kill you. Lung infections are usually indicated by coughing.

Common cold? There are many infections that initially indicate a normal cold but are not—they may be much more serious. At least call your doctor's office to get clearance before running. Be sure to explain how much you are running/walking, and what, if any medication you are taking.

Infections of the throat and above the neck—Most runners will be given the OK, but check with the doctor.

RISK OF SPEED

There is an increased risk of both injuries and cardiovascular events during speed sessions. Be sure to get your doctor's (usually phone) approval before beginning a speed program. The advice inside this book is generally conservative, but when in doubt, take more rest, more days off, and run slower. In other words...be more conservative.

YOUR
APPS

Chapter 4

PRACTICAL INFORMATION:
SHOES AND OTHER EQUIPMENT

In our increasingly complex world, running and walking offer an island of tranquility. Simplicity helps: Try to run from your house or office, using public streets or pedestrian walkways, wearing ordinary clothing. You don't need to join a country club or invest in expensive exercise equipment. While running/walking with another person can be motivating, most exercisers enjoy going alone, on most of their workouts. It helps, however, to have a "support team" as you go through the training (exercise companions, doctors, running shoe experts). You'll probably meet these folks through the "exercisers grapevine".

CONVENIENCE

Those who have a running course (park, etc.) near their home and office, are more likely to do the workouts on the schedule—when you need to do them.

SHOES: THE PRIMARY INVESTMENT—
USUALLY LESS THAN $100 AND MORE THAN $69

Most runners decide, wisely, to spend a little more time when choosing a good running shoe. After all, shoes are the only real equipment needed. When the design of the shoe matches the function and shape of your feet, running is easier. You'll also reduce blisters, foot fatigue and injuries.

Shoe shopping can be confusing. The best advice....is to get the best advice. The staff at a good running store can cut the time required and can usually lead you to a much better shoe choice than you would find yourself.

BUY THE TRAINING SHOE FIRST

Go to the running store in your area with the most experienced staff. First you'll need a pair for long runs and easy running days. Veterans may want to get a racing shoe (or lightweight training shoe) later. Bring along your most worn pair of shoes (any shoes), and a pair of running shoes that has worked well for you. Wait until you are several weeks into your training before you decide to get a racing shoe if you feel you need one.

WHO NEEDS A RACING SHOE?

In most cases, racing shoes only bestow a small improvement: a few seconds per mile. If this is what you need for your time goal, consider the racing models. Racing shoes tend to experience a breakdown in the mid-sole material earlier, and simply don't last as long as training shoes. Some of the very light models will compress during the latter stages of a 10K. Heavier runners will break the shoes down more quickly. After several weeks of use, if you feel that your training shoes are too heavy or "clunky" on faster runs, veterans can look at some lighter models. Most runners choose light weight training shoes because they last longer than racing shoes. After you have broken them in, you can use the lighter shoes during speed sessions and races.

A WATCH

There are a lot of good, inexpensive watches which will give you accurate times during speed workouts and races. Any watch that has a stopwatch function will do the job. Be sure to ask the staff person in the store how to use the stopwatch function. A few watches can make walk breaks easier by "beeping" after each running segment and then again after the walking segment. Of course, if you want to invest a little more, there are always more hi-tech smartwatches.

For more information on current watches that do this, go to www.RunInjuryFree.com.

CLOTHING: COMFORT ABOVE ALL

The "clothing thermometer" at the end of this book is a great guide. In the summer, you want to wear light, cool clothing. During cold weather, layering is the best strategy, and microfiber garments offer comfort and warmth.

But you don't have to have the latest techno-garments to run. On most days an old pair of shorts and a T-shirt are fine. As you get into the various components of your plan, you will find outfits that make you feel better and motivate you to get in your run even on bad weather days. It is also OK to give yourself a fashionable outfit as a "reward" for running/ walking regularly for several weeks.

A TRAINING JOURNAL

By using your journal to plan ahead (and then later, to review success and mistakes), you assume a major degree of control over your exercise future. You'll find it reinforcing to write down what you did each day, and miss that reinforcement when you skip. Be sure to read the training journal chapter, and you too, can steer yourself into enjoyment and success.

WHERE TO RUN/WALK

It helps to have several different venues for the various workouts. Try to find 2 or more options for each:

Long ones—scenic, interesting areas are best—with some pavement and some softer surface if possible. It helps to run some of your long ones on the course you plan to race.

Speed training and the "Magic Mile"—Only veterans who want to improve will be doing speedwork. A track is usually best, but an accurate GPS or accelerometer device can allow you to run these sessions almost anywhere.

Races—Look carefully at the course—avoid hills, too many turns, or even too much flat terrain if you usually train on rolling hills (in a non-hilly race, you will fatigue your flat running muscles more quickly, if you don't do the long ones on flat terrain). Read the section on racing.

Running drills—Any safe area with a secure surface

SAFETY—TOP PRIORITY!

Pick a course that is away from car traffic, and is in a safe area—where crime is unlikely. Try to have two or more options for each of the components because variety can be very motivating.

SURFACE

With the correct amount of cushion, and the selection of the right shoes for you, pavement should not give extra shock to the legs or body. A smooth surface dirt or gravel path, is best for most runners/walkers for the easy days. But beware of an uneven surface, especially if you have weak ankles or foot problems. For your time trials, speedwork, and drills, you may have to talk to your shoe experts to avoid blisters, etc. when exercising on certain types of surfaces. Watch the slanvt of the road, trail, track or sidewalk—flat is best.

PICKING AN EXERCISE COMPANION

On long ones and on easy days, don't go with someone who is faster than you—unless he or she is fully comfortable slowing down to an easy pace—that is...slow for you. It is motivating to go with someone who will go slow enough so that you can talk. Share stories, jokes, problems if you wish, and you'll bond together in a very positive way. The friendships forged on workouts can be the strongest and longest lasting—if you're not huffing and puffing (or puking) from trying to go at a pace that is too fast. On speed days, however, it sometimes helps to run with a faster person as long as you are running at the right pace for you.

REWARDS

Positive reinforcement works! Treating yourself to a smoothie after a hot or hard session, taking a cool dip in a pool, going out to a special restaurant after a longer one—all of these can reinforce the successful completion of another week or month. Of particular benefit is having a snack, within 30 minutes of the finish, that has about 200-300 calories, containing 80% carbohydrate and 20% protein. The products Accelerade and Endurox R4 are already formulated with this ratio for your convenience, and give you a recovery boost also.

AN APPOINTMENT ON THE CALENDAR

Write down each of your weekly runs, from the schedule in this book, at least one week in advance, on your calendar or journal. Since each week is broken down for you, you can use it as your guide. Sure you can change if you have to. But by having a secure slot, you will be able to plan for your workout, and make it happen. Pretend that this is an appointment with your boss, or your most important client, etc. Actually, you are your most important client!

MOTIVATION TO GET OUT THE DOOR

There are three times when exercisers feel challenged: 1) early in the morning, 2) after work, or 3) before the tough workouts. In the motivation section you'll find rehearsals for challenging situations. It'll be much easier to stay motivated once you experience a regular series of workouts that make you feel good. When you run/walk at the right pace, with the right preparation, you feel better, can relate to others better, and have more energy to enjoy the rest of the day. Enjoyment of exercise will increase your motivation.

TREADMILLS ARE JUST AS GOOD AS STREETS FOR SHORT SESSIONS

More and more runners/walkers are using treadmills for at least 50% of their workouts—particularly those who have small children. It is a fact that treadmills tend to tell you that you have gone further or faster than you really have (but usually are not off by more than 10%). But if you exercise on a treadmill for the number of minutes assigned, at the effort level you are used to (no huffing and puffing), you will get close enough to the training effect you wish. To ensure that you have covered enough miles, feel free to add 10% to your assigned mileage.

USUALLY NO NEED TO EAT BEFORE THE WORKOUT

Most exercisers don't need to eat before sessions that are less than an hour. The only exceptions are those with diabetes or severe blood sugar problems. Many feel better during a workout when they have enjoyed a cup of coffee about an hour before the start. Caffeine engages the central nervous system, which gets all of the systems needed for exercise up and running to capacity, very quickly.

If your blood sugar is low, which often occurs in the afternoon, it helps to have a snack of about 100-200 calories, about 30 minutes before exercise, which is composed of 80% carbohydrate and 20% protein. The Accelerade product has been very successful.

Chapter 5

THE GALLOWAY RUN-WALK-RUN METHOD

"Walk breaks let you control the amount of fatigue on your legs and body"

I doubt that you will find any training component that will help you in more ways than my run-walk-run method. I continue to be amazed, every week, at the reports of how these strategic walks help 5K and 10K runners to enjoy the racing experience more, as they improve the finish time. When placed appropriately for the individual, walk breaks will erase fatigue, reduce stress, improve motivation, increase running enjoyment, speed up recovery, and allow the runner to finish with strength. Here's how it works.

WALK BEFORE YOU GET TIRED

Most of us, even when untrained, can walk for several miles before fatigue sets in, because walking is an activity that we can do efficiently for hours. Running is more work, because you have to lift your body off the ground and then absorb the shock of the landing, over and over. The continuous use of the running muscles will produce much more fatigue, aches, and pains than running at the same pace while taking walk breaks. If you walk before your running muscles start to get tired, you allow the muscle to recover instantly—increasing your capacity for exercise while reducing the chance of next-day soreness.

The "method" part involves having a strategy. By using a ratio of running and walking that is adjusted for the pace per mile, you can manage your fatigue. Using this fatigue-reduction tool early gives you the muscle resources and the mental confidence to cope with the challenges that can come later. Even when you don't need the extra strength and resiliency bestowed by the method, you will feel better during and after your run, and finish knowing that you could have gone further.

"The run-walk-run method is very simple: you run for a short segment and then take a walk break, and keep repeating this pattern."

Walk breaks allow you to take control over fatigue, in advance, so that you can enjoy every run. By taking them early and often you can feel strong, even after a run that is very long for you. Beginners will alternate very short run segments with short walks. Even elite runners find that walk breaks on long runs allow them to recover faster. There is no need to be totally exhausted at the end of any long run.

Walk breaks....

- Give you control over the way you feel at the end

- Erase fatigue

- Push back your fatigue wall

- Allow for endorphins to collect during each walk break—you feel good!

- Break up the distance into manageable units ("two more minutes")

- Speed recovery

- Reduce the chance of aches, pains and injury

- Allow you to feel good afterward—carrying on the rest of your day without debilitating fatigue

- Give you all of the endurance of the distance of each session—without the pain

- Allow older runners or heavier runners to recover fast, and feel as good or better than the younger (slimmer) days

A SHORT AND GENTLE WALKING STRIDE

It's better to walk slowly, with a short stride. There has been some irritation of the shins, when runners or walkers maintain a stride that is too long. Relax and enjoy the walk.

NO NEED TO EVER ELIMINATE THE WALK BREAKS

Some beginners assume that they must work toward the day when they don't have to take any walk breaks at all. This is up to the individual, but is not recommended. Remember that you decide what ratio of run-walk-run to use. There is no rule that requires you to hold to any ratio on a given day. As you adjust the run-walk to how you feel, you gain control over your fatigue.

I've run for about 50 years, and I enjoy running more than ever because of walk breaks. Each run I take energizes my day. I would not be able to run almost every day if I didn't insert the walk breaks early and often. I start most runs taking a short walk break after a minute of running. By 2 miles I am usually walking every 3-4 minutes. By 5 miles the ratio often goes to every 7-10 minutes.

But there are days every year when I stay at 3 minutes and even a few days at 1 min. On long runs, however, I set my ratio to be about 20 seconds every minute or two—and stay with it throughout.

HOW TO KEEP TRACK OF THE WALK BREAKS

There are several watches, and now smartwatches, which can be set to beep when it's time to walk, and then beep again when it's time to start up again. Check our website (www.jeffgalloway.com) or a good running store for advice in this area.

WALK BREAKS ON LONG RUNS AND DURING 5K/10K RACES

Longer long runs allow you to run faster in 5K and 10K races. Walk breaks speed up recovery so that even after a 15-mile training run, you can run a hard speed workout in a few days. Walk breaks can be taken according to the following schedule. Feel free to walk more or to cut both of the segments in half, for example: 1 min run/2 min walk could be converted to 30 seconds run/60 seconds walk.

Note: If you're feeling strong in the last mile, you can run as much as you wish.

Run pace (minutes/mile)	Minutes running/Minutes walking
8:00	Run 4 min/Walk 30 sec
8:30	Run 3 min/Walk 30 sec
9:00	Run 2 min/Walk 30 sec
10:00	Run 1:30 min/Walk 30 sec
11:00-12:00	Run 1 min/Walk 30 sec
13:00-14:00	Run 30 sec/Walk 30 sec OR 20/20 OR 15/15
15:00	Run 15 sec/Walk 30 sec
16:00	Run 10 sec/Walk 30 sec

Chapter 6

THE MAGIC MILE GIVES YOU A REALISTIC GOAL AND PACE

In this chapter 5K and 10K runners will learn how to determine a realistic pace on long runs and in the race. Veterans will see how much improvement can be expected, and whether they are on track for the goal at various times in the training program. As you approach your goal at the end of the program, you can use the "Galloway Performance Predictor" to determine what you will be capable of running in your race—and how to make adjustments for temperature.

PREDICTION STRATEGY

More than 20 years ago, I started using a one mile time trial (called a "magic mile" or MM) as a prediction tool. After working with thousands of runners, I've found that those who do at least four of these during a season can gain a very realistic prediction of their current racing potential. The time you record from this one mile time trial will predict your current performance potential: Add 33 seconds to the MM for your fast one-mile average in the 5K and multiply MM time by 1.15 for the 10K predicted pace per mile.

LONG RUN PACE: YOU CANNOT RUN TOO SLOW!

Slow your pace by at least 3 minutes and 30 seconds per mile from the time predicted in your goal race by the magic mile (See following section). Slow down further by 30 seconds a mile for every 5 degrees above 60°F. It's always better to slow down more than this. Because you have scheduled speed sessions a few days after some of the long runs, even slower long runs will help you recover faster while producing all of the endurance.

In order to run the time in the race indicated by Galloway's Performance Predictor:

- You must do the training necessary for the goal—according to the 5K and 10K training programs in this book

- You must not be injured

- You must run with an even-paced effort

- The weather on goal race day is not adverse: ideal is below 60°F (or 14°C), no strong headwinds, no heavy rain or snow, etc.

- There are no crowds to run through, (crowds force you to run farther than race distance), or hills.

HOW TO DO THE "MAGIC MILE" TIME TRIAL (MM)

1. Go to a track, or other accurately measured course. One mile is 4 laps around a track.

2. Warm up by walking for 5 minutes, then running a minute and walking a minute, then jogging an easy 800 meter (half mile or two laps around a track).

3. Do 4 acceleration-gliders. If desired, you can do 4 cadence drills (both are described in the "Drills" chapter).

4. Walk for 3-4 minutes

5. Start your measured mile at a normal running pace and within 50 to 100 steps increase up to a fast pace for you (but not all-out). Use walk break suggestions in this chapter, or run the way you want. Keep the watch running even on walk breaks and stop it after the 4th lap.

6. *On your first MM, don't run all-out from the start—just run faster than you usually run.*

7. Cool down by reversing the warm-up.

8. A school track is the best venue. Don't use treadmills because they tend to be notoriously uncalibrated, and often tell you that you ran farther or faster than you really did. Most of the GPS or Accelerometer devices will provide a fairly accurate measurement—but the track is best.

9. On each successive MM, try to adjust pace in order to run a faster time on each successive one.

10. Use the Performance Predictor to see what time is predicted in the goal race.

HOW HARD SHOULD I RUN THE MM—AFTER THE FIRST ONE?

With each successive MM, pick up the pace in order to better the previous best time. By the fourth or fifth one, you should be running fairly close to your potential. Most runners I've worked with continue to improve throughout the training program on most (but not all) of the MMs.

Run the first lap slightly slower than you think you can average. Take a short walk break as noted in the run-walk-run suggestions in this chapter, if you wish. If you aren't huffing and puffing you can pick up the pace a bit on second lap. If you are huffing after the first lap, then just hold your pace during lap two—or reduce it slightly. Most runners benefit from taking a walk break after the second lap. At the end of lap 3, the walk break is optional. It is OK to be breathing hard on the last lap. If you are slowing down on the last lap, start a little slower on the next MM. When you finish, you should feel like you couldn't run more than about half a lap further at that pace (if that). You may find that you don't need many walk breaks during the MM test—experiment and adjust. Don't sprint at the end, as this can produce injury.

GALLOWAY'S PERFORMANCE PREDICTOR

Step 1:
Run your "magic mile" time trial (4 laps around the track)

Step 2a:
Compute your current per mile pace in a hard 5K by adding 33 seconds

Step 2b:
Compute your current per mile pace in a hard 10K by multiplying by 1.15

Suggested long-run pace:

Add 3:30 minutes to predicted 5K or 10K pace. You may run slower than this if you wish.

Example:

Mile time: 10:00
5K current ability:
add 33 seconds = 10:33 pace per mile in a hard 5K race.

10K current ability:

multiply by 1.15 = 11:30 pace per mile in a hard 10K race.

For a long run pace suggestion, add 3:30 min per mile:

15:00 minutes per mile for 10K
14:03 minutes per mile for the 5K
(it's always OK to run slower than this)

One Mile Time	(+ 33 seconds) FAST 5K Pace	(multiply by 1.15) FAST 10K Pace	(add about 3 min per mile to 10K pace) Long-Run Training Pace
5:00	5:33	5:45	8:45
5:30	6:03	6:19	9:30
6:00	6:33	6:54	10:00
6:30	7:03	7:28	10:30
7:00	7:33	8:03	11:00
7:30	8:03	8:38	11:30
8:00	8:33	9:12	12:00
8:30	9:03	9:47	12:45
9:00	9:33	10:21	13:30
9:30	10:03	10:55	14:00
10:00	10:33	11:30	14:30

10:30	11:03	12:05	15:00
11:00	11:33	12:39	15:40
11:30	12:03	13:14	16:15
12:00	12:33	13:48	17:00
12:30	13:03	14:23	17:30
13:00	13:33	15:00	18:00
13:30	14:03	15:33	18:30
14:00	14:33	16:06	19:00
14:30	15:33	16:40	20:00
15:00	15:33	17:15	20:15
15:30	16:33	17:50	21:00
16:00	16:33	18:24	21:30

Note: The 1.15 multiplier (for a 10K predictions) assumes that you will be running about all-out effort by the end of the race.

Walkbreaks in the MM? It is your choice. Most find that at least a short walk of 10-20 seconds at the half helps improve time.

FIRST-TIME 5K/10K RACERS—RUN TO FINISH ONLY

I strongly recommend that first-time racers not attempt a time goal. During the race itself, I recommend running the first half at your training pace. During the last half you may run as you wish.

TIME GOAL RUNNERS MAY MAKE A "LEAP OF FAITH" GOAL PREDICTION

I have no problem letting my e-coach athletes, who've run one or more races at the current goal distance, choose a goal time that is faster than that predicted by the MM. As you do the speed training, and the long runs, you should improve...but how much? In my experience this "leap of faith" should not exceed 3-5% improvement in a three-month training program.

1. Run the MM

2. Use the formula above to predict what you could run now, if you were trained for a 5K/10K race

3. Choose the amount of improvement during the training program (3-5%)

4. Subtract this from step 2—this is your goal time

| | (Over a 2-3 month training program) | |
First prediction	3% Improvement	5% Improvement
20 minutes/mi	36 sec/mi	1 minute/mi
18 minutes/mi	33 seconds/mi	54 seconds/mi
16 minutes/mi	27 seconds/mi	48 seconds/mi
14 minutes/mi	25 seconds/mi	42 seconds/mi
12 minutes/mi	21 seconds/mi	36 seconds/mi
10 minutes/mi	18 seconds/mi	30 seconds/mi
9 minutes/mi	16 seconds/mi	27 seconds/mi
8 minutes/mi	14 seconds/mi	24 seconds/mi
7 minutes/mi	12 seconds/mi	21 seconds/mi

The key to goal setting is keeping your ego in check. From my experience, I have found that a 3% improvement is realistic. This means that if your initial 5K or 10K time prediction is 10 min/mi, it is realistic to assume that you could lower it by about 20 sec a mile if you do the speed training and the long runs as noted in my training schedules.

Those who have been running longer (two years or more) and have no injuries could try for a more aggressive, 5% improvement: 30 sec/mi at 10 min pace.

In all of these situations, however, everything must come together to produce the predicted result. You prepare your legs and feet for the physiological and mechanical effort by doing the speed work necessary for your goal. Read the speed chapter and the training program chapters to see how this works.

REASONS WHY YOU MAY NOT BE IMPROVING

1. You're overtrained, and tired—if so, reduce your training, and/or take an extra rest day.

2. You may have chosen a goal that is too ambitious for your current ability.

3. You may have missed some of your workouts, or not been as regular with your training.

4. The temperature may have been above 60°F (14°C). Above this, you will slow down.

5. When using different test courses, one of them may not have been accurately measured, or contain more hills, headwinds, etc.

Final reality check

The last two MMs are crucial for predicting your race pace. You may pick your fastest time from the MMs to get a good prediction in your goal race.

Use a journal!

Record your MMs and the quarter-mile "splits" if you can remember them. This allows you to adjust your pace on each successive MM.

Chapter 7

PRE-SEASON CONDITIONING

WHAT YOU NEED TO KNOW BEFORE STARTING THIS PROGRAM

- Having been walking regularly for 3 weeks

- A minimum of 3 days a week—15 min each session, or more

- No injuries or ailments that would prevent strenuous training

- Be sure to tell your doctor what you are planning to do, and get his or her blessing before starting

Note: The following is a training program for walkers and runners. This assumes that the individual is starting from zero running. If you have been doing three months of regular but slow running, you could jump in to the schedule at the distance of your current long run. Example: a walker or runner who has been covering 2 miles on the weekends could start at week 6. Veteran 5K and 10K runners whose long runs are up to the distances in the schedule, can start with the first week in the schedule.

CONDITIONING PROGRAM

Mon	Tues	Wed	Thu	Fri	Sat	Sun
Week 1 (Walkers will walk only, runners will run for 5 seconds/walk for 55 seconds on the run/walk days)						
10 min run/walk	15 min walk	13 min run/walk	18 min walk	off	1 mile run/walk	off/walk
Week 2 (Walkers will walk only, runners will run for 5 seconds/walk for 55 seconds on the run/walk days)						
15 min run/walk	20 min walk	17 min run/walk	22 min walk	off	1.25 mi run/walk	off/walk
Week 3 (Walkers will walk only, runners will run for 10 seconds/walk for 50 seconds on the run/walk days)						
19 min run/walk	24 min walk	21 min run/walk	26 min walk	off	1.5 mi run/walk	off/walk
Week 4 (Walkers will walk only, runners will run for 10 seconds/walk for 50 seconds on the run/walk days)						
23 min run/walk	28 min walk	25 min run/walk	30 min walk	off	1.75 mi run/walk	off/walk
Week 5 (Walkers will walk only, runners will run for 10 seconds/walk for 50 seconds on the run/walk days)						
27 min run/walk	30 min walk	29 min run/walk	30 min walk	off	2 mi run/walk	off/walk
Week 6 (Walkers will walk only, runners will run for 15 seconds/walk for 45 seconds on the run/walk days)						
30 min run/walk	30 min walk	30 min run/walk	30 min walk	off	2.25 mi run/walk	off/walk
Week 7 (Walkers will walk only, runners will run for 15 seconds/walk for 45 seconds on the run/walk days)						
30 min run/walk	30 min walk	30 min run/walk	30 min walk	off	2.5 mi run/walk	off/walk
Week 8 (Walkers will walk only, runners will run for 15 seconds/walk for 45 seconds on the run/walk days)						
30 min run/walk	30 min walk	30 min run/walk	30 min walk	off	2.75 mi run/walk	off/walk

Note: If you need several weeks at each run-walk ratio level, take it. This preconditioning training should not be stressful or painful. When in doubt, ease off.

"TO FINISH" TRAINING PROGRAMS

These schedules are designed for those who are running their first 5K or 10K, or for anyone who just wants to finish. Before beginning the following schedule, the long run should be within one mile of the distance of the first long one on the schedule. Your other runs should also be about 30 minutes or more, twice a week. The conditioning schedule in the last chapter allows for a conservative buildup if you are not running this amount.

SYMBOLS

(xx = run the long run 3.5 min/mi slower than your magic mile predicts in the 10K, adjust for temperature)

(MM = "magic mile", which is run in the middle of the running time for that day)

5K—TO FINISH

Runners who are already running more than indicated can continue with their ratio of run-walk-run or continuous running.

Mon	Tues	Wed	Thu	Fri	Sat (xx)	Sun
Week 1 (Walkers will walk only, runners will run for 15 seconds/walk for 45 seconds on the run/walk days)						
30 min run/walk	30 min walk	30 min run/walk	30 min walk	off	3 mi	off/walk
Week 2 (Walkers will walk only, runners will run for 15 seconds/walk for 45 seconds on the run/walk days)						
30 min run/walk	30 min walk	30 min run/walk	30 min walk	off	3.5 mi run/walk	off/walk
Week 3 (Walkers will walk only, runners will run for 20 seconds/walk for 40 seconds on the run/walk days)						
30 min run/walk	30 min walk	30 min run/walk	30 min walk	off	2 mi with MM	off/walk
Week 4 (Walkers will walk only, runners will run for 20 seconds/walk for 40 seconds on the run/walk days)						
30 min run/walk	30 min walk	30 min run/walk	30 min walk	off	4 mi run/walk	off/walk
Week 5 (Walkers will walk only, runners will run for 25 seconds/walk for 35 seconds on the run/walk days)						
30 min run/walk	30 min walk	30 min run/walk	30 min walk	off	2 mi with MM	off/walk
Week 6 (Walkers will walk only, runners will run for 25 seconds/walk for 35 seconds on the run/walk days)						
30 min run/walk	30 min walk	30 min run/walk	30 min walk	off	4.5 mi run/walk	off/walk
Week 7 (Walkers will walk only, runners will run for 30 seconds/walk for 30 seconds on the run/walk days)						
30 min run/walk	30 min walk	30 min run/walk	30 min walk	off	Goal Race	off/walk

10K—TO FINISH

Runners who are already running more than indicated can continue with their ratio of run-walk-run or continuous running.

Mon	Tues	Wed	Thu	Fri	Sat	Sun
Week 1 (Walkers will walk only, runners will run for 15 seconds/walk for 45 seconds on the run/walk days)						
30 min run/walk	30 min walk	30 min run/walk	30 min walk	off	3 mi run/walk	off/walk
Week 2 (Walkers will walk only, runners will run for 15 seconds/walk for 45 seconds on the run/walk days)						
30 min run/walk	30 min walk	30 min run/walk	30 min walk	off	3.5 mi run/walk	off/walk
Week 3 (Walkers will walk only, runners will run for 15 seconds/walk for 45 seconds on the run/walk days)						
30 min run/walk	30 min walk	30 min run/walk	30 min walk	off	4 mi run/walk	off/walk
Week 4 (Walkers will walk only, runners will run for 20 seconds/walk for 40 seconds on the run/walk days)						
30 min run/walk	30 min walk	30 min run/walk	30 min walk	off	3 mi with MM	off/walk
Week 5 (Walkers will walk only, runners will run for 20 seconds/walk for 40 seconds on the run/walk days)						
30 min run/walk	30 min walk	30 min run/walk	30 min walk	off	4.5 mi run/walk	off/walk
Week 6 (Walkers will walk only, runners will run for 20 seconds/walk for 40 seconds on the run/walk days)						
30 min run/walk	30 min walk	30 min run/walk	30 min walk	off	5 mi run/walk	off/walk
Week 7 (Walkers will walk only, runners will run for 20 seconds/walk for 40 seconds on the run/walk days)						
30 min run/walk	30 min walk	30 min run/walk	30 min walk	off	3 mi with MM	off/walk

Week 8 (Walkers will walk only, runners will run for 25 seconds/walk for 35 seconds on the run/walk days)

30 min run/walk	30 min walk	30 min run/walk	30 min walk	off	5.5 mi run/walk	off/walk

Week 9 (Walkers, walk only, Runners will run for 25 seconds/walk for 35 seconds on the run/walk days)

30 min run/walk	30 min walk	30 min run/walk	30 min walk	off	3 mi with MM	off/walk

Week 10 (Walkers, walk only. Runners will run for 25 seconds/walk for 35 seconds on the run/walk days)

30 min run/walk	30 min walk	30 min run/walk	30 min walk	off	6 mi run/walk	off/walk

Week 11 (Walkers, walk only. Runners will run for 25 seconds/walk for 35 seconds on the run/walk days)

30 min run/walk	30 min walk	30 min run/walk	30 min walk	off	3 mi with MM	off/walk

Week 12 (Walkers, walk only. Runners will run for 25 seconds/walk for 35 seconds on the run/walk days)

30 min run/walk	30 min walk	30 min run/walk	30 min walk	off	6.5 mi run/walk	off/walk

Week 13 (Walkers, walk only. Runners will run for 30 seconds/walk for 30 seconds on the run/walk days)

30 min run/walk	30 min walk	30 min run/walk	30 min walk	off	3 mi run/walk	off/walk

Week 14 (Walkers, walk only. Runners will run for 30 seconds/walk for 30 seconds on the run/walk days)

30 min run/walk	30 min walk	30 min run/walk	30 min walk	off	Goal 10K	off/walk

Chapter 9

TIME GOAL PROGRAMS—
IF YOU'VE RUN A 5K OR 10K

ISSUES TO CONSIDER

If this is your first time doing speed training….

Be sure to ease into the faster running. Do the first two speed sessions much slower than you could run on that day. Then, ease into the training needed for your goal. Don't continue to run when you feel pain, but stop the workout immediately.

400 m is approximately a quarter of a mile or one lap around a track
1 mi is one mile, or 4 laps around a track

Following are several different components that are like the elements of sound in a symphony. Each one helps to develop and fine-tune your ease of running, endurance, and speed. The result can be a blending of heart and legs, left brain and right, and body-mind-spirit into an integrated unit.

Why can't I run faster now? Time improvement is a very complex process that is influenced by many factors beyond our control. The best approach is to stay focused on the goal and stay with the program that is realistic for you. By getting a reality check on your goals you can avoid pushing yourself beyond your limits.

Time challenged? The training programs don't have to take a lot of time, or produce debilitating fatigue. If you are experiencing any of these, you should stop doing the speed workouts and make adjustments. The methods in this book have been used successfully by thousands of runners. Some inherited athletic ability, but most did not. Most did not have much time to train. The schedules offer the minimum amount of work to prepare you for your goal.

Warning: you may experience addiction. I've noticed that there is a competitor hidden inside even the most sedentary person. *Something* inside us wants us to be more fit, and once we've established a base, that something wants us to push a little. After several more months of tests, the same internal programming can lead us to become the best we can be. I wrote more about this in GALLOWAY'S BOOK ON RUNNING.

The process of gently and regularly challenging yourself stimulates a desire to question priorities, use time and energy more efficiently, and extend your capabilities. This can work its way into other areas of life. Once you realize the benefits, you don't want to go back to lazier days. There are worse addictions.

Learn your limits. Most runners who start speedwork don't know how to do this safely. The series of gentle running improvement components in this book can lead you into a series of unknowns. I will give you the tools that give you a major amount of control over the process. The training progression involves guessing and adjusting, going just a little harder than the last workout, and then rebuilding stronger through planned rest/recovery. When done each week, the body makes continuous adaptations of improvement: farther, faster, smoother, and mentally tougher. You'll improve pace judgement, and learn when you can push harder or reduce effort, and intuitively fine-tune the movement of feet and legs. The solving of unexpected problems progressively reduces anxiety of the unknown as it develops confidence in confronting future challenges in other areas of life.

Beware of the ego. Some of the most timid beginning runners have become some of the most aggressive competitors I've worked with. As you experience time improvement through a well-designed training plan, the ego tells you things you want to hear. "If you improved 10 seconds with one weekly speed workout, two hard workouts will double the improvement." Many runners have let the ego take away their enjoyment of a gentle run—pushing them farther and faster on days that should have been reserved for slow recovery. Once they started racing, the ego told them that lap times in workouts or in races could bestow greater satisfaction. Beware of this line of thinking. The fatigue-induced slower race times will trigger disappointment, while faster times most often lead to a yearning for even faster times.

It is healthy to let your ego have its moments of glory as you perform well. Improvement is not a continuous upward curve, and the ego has a problem with any downturn. A natural selection process occurs during a speed training season, as the ego is forced to deal with reality, and make adjustments. But by maintaining the enjoyment of a fun run every week, and appreciating the afterglow from any run, you can receive a balanced set of rewards, while keeping the ego in check.

While training for faster times can keep you focused, and may improve motivation, the blending of mind body and spirit is maintained primarily through enjoying of the act of running. Be sure to include enough slow runs, warm up and cool down slowly, and take walk breaks from the beginning of the run. Even when I was training for the Olympics, about 90% of my weekly miles were spent running at a slow and enjoyable pace.

Performance increase is not a continuous upward trek. Be prepared to record times on at least half of your races that are slower than you think you should be running. This is often due to the ego telling you to run faster than you are really able to at that point in time. Be patient, learn from your setbacks, and you will generally move forward.

EVERY OTHER DAY?

If you are already running more than 3 days a week, and are not experiencing any fatigue or injury issues, you can certainly continue with the number of days that work into your schedule. Be careful, however. Speed training, and the drills in this program will stress your muscles, tendons, motivation, etc. more than ever. When in doubt, back off and run the following schedule. If you are running more than three days a week, make sure that you take it very easy between each workout. I strongly suggest that you take a day off from running before the speed workouts, before long runs, and before races.

CHANGING THE SPECIFIC WORKOUT DAYS

It's fine to shift the days around to accommodate your lifestyle. Just try to be consistent in your shifting, and take the day off from exercise before a long run, a speed workout or a race.

HOW SLOW FOR THE LONG RUNS—
AND HOW OFTEN THE WALK BREAKS

Long runs should be run at least 3.5 min/mi slower than your predicted 10K goal pace. Feel free to run slower than this. See the chapter on "Choosing The Right Goal" in this book.

WALK BREAKS ON LONG RUNS

Walk breaks can be taken according to the following schedule. Feel free to walk more or to cut both of the segments in half, for example: 2 min run/1 min walk could be converted to 60 seconds run/30 seconds walk.

Run pace (minutes/mile)	Minutes running/Minutes walking
8:00	Run 4 min/Walk 30 sec
8:30	Run 3 min/Walk 30 sec
9:00	Run 2 min/Walk 30 sec
10:00	Run 1:30 min/Walk 30 sec
11:00-12:00	Run 1 min/Walk 30 sec
13:00-14:00	Run 30 sec/Walk 30 sec OR 20/20 OR 15/15
15:00	Run 15 sec/Walk 30 sec
16:00	Run 10 sec/Walk 30 sec

WARM UP (AND COOL DOWN) BEFORE MAGIC MILE, SPEED DAY WORKOUTS, AND RACES

Here is a format that will get your mind and body ready to go faster. As you go through the training, fine-tune this to work for your specific needs. Then use the final product as your warm-up before the goal race.

The cool-down should be a reversal of the warm-up. Never jump into your car, shower, or stand around right after running. There is a cardiac risk in doing this.

1. Walk slowly for 5 minutes

2. Run for a few seconds and walk a minute for 10 minutes

3. Jog slowly for 10 minutes

4. Walk for 3-4 minutes

5. Do a cadence drill (4-8 of them) see the "Drill" chapter for details

6. Walk for 1-3 minutes

7. Do an acceleration-glider drill (4-8) see the "Drill chapter for details

8. Walk for 5 minutes

9. Start the workout

WALK BREAKS ON RACE REHEARSAL DAYS

On the race rehearsal segments, use the walk break strategy you plan to use in the race itself.

WHAT IF YOUR MMS PREDICT A RACE PACE THAT IS SLOWER THAN YOUR GOAL?

As you near the end of the program, see how close you are to your projected goal by using the "Galloway Performance Predictor". If your predictions are a few seconds off your "leap of faith" goal, it's OK to continue to train for your original goal. In the goal race, a safe strategy is to start the race at the pace predicted by your MMs (as an average of your last two MMs). If you have something left (and this often happens), go for the goal at the half way point in the goal race.

PRIMARY TRAINING COMPONENTS

Long runs—Run these very slowly, at least 3:30 min/mi slower than you could run in your goal race as predicted by your one mile TT. Put in the walk breaks that are suggested in the Run-Walk-Run chapter in this book—or more often than recommended. I have not found anyone who has run the long runs too slowly or has taken the walk breaks too often. Slower long runs build the same endurance as fast long runs—with little or no risk of injury or burnout.

Drills—Cadence Drills (CD) and Acceleration-Gliders (Acg). These easy exercises teach your body to improve form and running mechanics. They are not exhausting—most runners say they energize an average run. Doing 4-8 of each drill, once a week, will improve speed and running efficiency.

Hills build strength better than any other training component. Warm up by jogging slowly for a half mile. Then, do 4 acceleration-gliders (Acg). Start each hill at a jog, and pick up the turnover as you go over the top of the hill. Don't sprint, but you will be huffing and puffing. Shorten stride as you go up the hill to keep the leg muscles resilient. See the section in this book on hill training.

Magic Mile time trials (MM)—These are done every few weeks to monitor progress and overtraining.

- Go to a track, or other accurately measured course.
- Warm up by walking for 5 minutes, then running a minute and walking a minute, then jogging an easy 800 meter (half mile or two laps around a track)
- Do 4 acceleration-gliders. These are listed in the "Drills" chapter.
- Walk for 3-4 minutes
- Run the 1 mile MM—a hard effort. Follow the walk break suggestions.
- On your first MM, don't run all-out from the start—ease into your pace after the first third of the distance.
- Cool down by reversing the warm-up.

- A school track is the best venue. Don't use a treadmill because they tend to be notoriously uncalibrated, and often tell you that you ran farther or faster than you really did. Run the first lap slightly slower than you think you can average. Take a short walk break as noted in the walk break suggestions in this chapter. It is OK to be huffing and puffing on the last lap. If you are slowing down on the last lap, start a little slower on the next one. When you finish your last few MMs, you should feel like you couldn't run more than about half a lap further at that pace (if that).

- Keep walking after the MM.

RACE REHEARSAL (RR)

The workouts listed on RR days will prepare you for pacing during your goal race. Look at your watch at the end of each lap, with the goal of hitting the exact time needed. During these RR workout days, you'll be doing 2 segments. After the first segment, walk for at least 5 minutes (no more than 10 minutes) and then do the second segment about 1-2 seconds per lap faster than goal pace if you can do this without struggling. If there is some struggling, slow down to goal pace. Each lap on a standard track is 400 meters. If you cannot maintain pace (especially due to heat), break up the workout into more segments. For example, on Monday of week 4 in the 5K program, there is a 2 mile scheduled at race pace, followed by an 800 meter as the second segment. If you start to slow down on the first lap of the second segment, stop, walk for 3 minutes and run another 400. Try to run the portions about 1-2 seconds per lap faster than goal pace. You may also break up the second segment into 200 meter segments if you need to.

HILLS (H) BUILD STRENGTH

Hill training will help you maximize the strength needed for running 5Ks and 10Ks. Doing a few hills, before the start of the speed training season will strengthen the legs for running better than any exercise or equipment. Hill repeats will produce muscles that have a higher capacity to perform—in speed training and in a race.

HILL WORKOUT

Done on a Thursday, by time goal runners. Warm up as before a speed workout. Pick a hill that is not steep at all. If it is too easy after the first workout, pick a slightly steeper hill. Run up at approximately goal pace, slightly over the top, and walk down. Never strain or run all out. Number of hills are noted (2H) meaning "2 hill repeats"). Before each hill count down from the top, the number of walking steps as follows:

- First time—50 walking steps

- Have done some speed training—100-150 walking steps

- Advanced speed trainers—200-300 walking steps

See also the "hill running form" segment of the running form chapter.

Note: It is always better to stay smooth and not struggle at the end of all workouts.

SPEED DAYS

After a warm-up, you'll be running a series of 400 meter repetitions, followed by a walk of 200 meters. A 400 meter is one lap around a track or a quarter mile. Each of these segments should be run 8 seconds faster than you want to run a quarter of a mile in the race itself. For example, if your goal pace is 8 min/mile, then each quarter mile in the race would need to be 2 min each. So the goal time for each 400 in the workout is 1:52. Walk for 2-3 minutes (or 200 meters) and repeat the process. Speed days are presented in more detail in a later chapter.

Note: Even experienced runners increase injury risk when they incorporate speed training. Be sensitive to all "weak link" areas and cut back according to the injury section of the book. Do not continue to do the workout if there is a chance of having done something that could initiate an injury.

REST DAYS

As you increase the distance and speed sessions, it's best to take days off from running as noted in the schedules. There is very little to be gained by running a short distance on rest days. Experienced runners who normally run more than 3 days a week can run very easily for 30-40 min on Thursdays.

5K SCHEDULES

Note: Speedwork increases injury risk . You'll reduce this risk to minimal levels by gradually increasing the number of repetitions, inserting adequate rest, and being sensitive to all "weak link" areas. These are the places that tend to get sore or painful when you run farther or faster than you have been running. When in doubt, don't run as fast, increasing the rest between repetitions and between workouts. If you even suspect that you may have the beginning of an injury, stop the workout immediately.

Symbols: (* = cadence drill) (** = acceleration glider) See the "Drills" chapter in this book (xx = run the long run at least 3:30 min/mi slower than your magic mile predicts in the 5K, adjust for temperature)
(RR = "Race Rehearsal": you will be running at goal pace, gradually increasing the distance)
(MM = "Magic Mile", which is run in the middle of the running time for that day)
(XT means "cross-training" or alternative exercise such as walking, cycling, swimming, water running)

Note: During the RR segments, practice the run-walk-run ratio you wish to use in the race itself.

(H = hill repeats, done on Thursday, described above in primary training components)

TIME GOAL 5K: 15:00

- Wednesday's speed workout of 400 repetitions should be run at 1:06 each

- Long runs should be run no faster than 8:15 min per mile (for quick recovery), adjust for temperature

- Total mileage for MM days is listed with "total" at end

- Try to stay smooth at the end of the speed session, even when tired; it's OK to slow down a second or two

Mon	Tues	Wed	Thu	Fri	Sat	Sun
Week 1						
MM (*/**) 4 mi total	Walk 30 min or XT or off	Speed Day (*/**) 6 x 400	5K easy (2H)	off	Long run 5 mi (8K) xx	off
Week 2						
RR (*/**) 1.5 mi (7:15) plus 1200 meter 1:10 per lap	Walk 30 min or XT or off	Speed Day 8 x 400 (*/**)	5K easy (3H)	off	Long run 6.5 mi (11K) xx	off
Week 3						
MM (*/**) 6 mi total (13.5K) xx	Walk 30 min or XT or off	Speed Day (*/**) 10 x 400	5K easy (4H)	off	Long run 8 mi	off
Week 4						
RR 2 mi (9:36) plus 800 meters (*/**) 1:12 per lap	Walk 30 min or XT or off	Speed Day 12 x 400 (*/**)	5K easy (3H)	off	Long run 10 mi (16K) xx	off
Week 5						
MM (*/**)	Walk 30 min or off	Speed Day 14 x 400	5K easy (2H)	off	Long: (19K)	off
Week 6						
16 x 400	Walk 30 min or XT or off	(*/**) 6 x 400	5K easy (2H)	off	RR 2.25 mi (10:48) 5 mi total (*/**)	off
Goal Race Week						
3-4 x 400 (1:09) 4 mi total (*/**)	XT or off	4 mi total (*/**)	5K easy	off	Goal Race	

TIME GOAL 5K: 17:30

- Wednesday's speed workout of 400 repetitions should be run at 1:16 each

- Long runs should be run no faster than 9:00 min per mile (for quick recovery), adjust for temperature

- Goal times for Monday's RR time trials are in parentheses

- Total mileage for MM days is listed with "total" at end (MM is embedded in the middle)

- Try to stay smooth at the end of the speed session, even when tired; it's OK to slow down a second or two

Mon	Tues	Wed	Thu	Fri	Sat	Sun
Week 1						
MM (*/**) 4 mi total	Walk 30 min or XT or off	Speed Day (*/**) 6 x 400	5K easy (2H)	off	Long run 5 mi (8K) xx	off
Week 2						
RR (*/**) 1.5 mi (8:29) plus 1200 meter (1:22 per lap)	Walk 30 min or XT or off	Speed Day 8 x 400 (*/**)	5K easy (3H)	off	Long run 6.5 mi (11K) xx	off
Week 3						
MM (*/**) 5 mi total	Walk 30 min or XT or off	Speed Day (*/**) 10 x 400	5K easy (4H)	off	Long run 8 mi (13.5K) xx	off
Week 4						
RR (*/**) 2 mi (11:17) plus 800 meters (1:22 per lap)	Walk 30 min or XT or off	Speed Day 12 x 400 (*/**)	5K easy (3H)	off	Long run 5 mi (8K) xx	off
Week 5						
MM (*/**) 6 mi total	Walk 30 min or XT	Speed Day (*/**)	5K easy (2H)	off	10 mi (16K)	off
Week 6						
16 x 400 (*/**)	Walk 30 min or XT or off	4 x 400 (*/**)	5K easy (2H)	off	2.25 mi RR (12:41) (*/**)	off
Next week: Goal Race						
3-4 x 400 (*/**)	XT or off	3-4 x 400 (*/**)	5K easy	off	Goal Race	

TIME GOAL 5K: 19:59

- Wednesday's speed Workout of 400 repetitions should be run at 1:28 each

- Long runs should be run no faster than 10:00 min per mile (for quick recovery), adjust for temperature

- Goal times for Monday's RR time trials are in parentheses

- Total mileage for MM days is listed with "total" at end (MM is embedded in the middle)

- Try to stay smooth at the end of the speed session, even when tired; it's OK to slow down a second or two

Mon	Tues	Wed	Thu	Fri	Sat	Sun
Week 1						
MM (*/**) 4 mi total	Walk 30 min or XT or off	Speed Day (*/**) 8 x 400	5K easy(2H)	off	Long run 5 mi (8K) xx	off
Week 2						
RR (*/**) 1.5mi (9:40) plus 1200 meter (1:30 per lap)	Walk 30 min or XT or off	Speed Day 10 x 400 (*/**)	5K easy(3H)	off	Long run 6.5 mi (11K) xx	off
Week 3						
MM (*/**) 5 mi total	Walk 30 min or XT or off	Speed Day (*/**) 12 x 400	5K easy(3H)	off	Long run 8 mi (13.5K) xx	off
Week 4						
RR (*/**) 2 mi (12:54) plus 800 meters (1:34 per lap)	Walk 30 min or XT or off	Speed Day 14 x 400	5K easy(2H)	off	2 mi RR (13:25)	off
Week 5						
MM (*/**) 6 mi total	Walk 30 min or XT or off	16 x 400 (*/**)	5K easy(2H)	off	11 mi (17.5K)	off
Week 6						
6 x 400(*/**)	Walk 30 min or XT or off	4 x 400 (*/**)	5K easy(2H)	off	2.25 mi RR (14:30) (*/**)	off
Next week: Goal Race						
3-4 x 400 (*/**)	XT or off	3-4 x 400 (*/**)	5K easy or XT or off	off	Goal Race	

TIME GOAL 5K: 23:59

- Wednesday's speed 400 repetitions should be run at 1:44 each

- Long runs should be run no faster than 11:15 per mile for quick recovery, adjust for temperature.

- Goal times for Monday's RR time trials are in parentheses

- Total mileage for MM days is listed with "total" at end

- Try to stay smooth at the end of the speed session, even when tired; it's OK to slow down a second or two

Mon	Tues	Wed	Thu	Fri	Sat	Sun
Week 1						
MM (*/**) 4 mi total	Walk 30 min or XT or off	Speed Day (*/**) 7 x 400	5K easy(1H)	off	Long run 4 mi (6.5K) xx	off
Week 2						
RR (*/**) 1.5 mi (11:37) plus 1200 meter (1:55 per lap)	Walk 30 min or XT or off	Speed Day 9 x 400 (*/**)	5K easy(2H)	off	Long run 5.5 mi (9K) xx	off
Week 3						
MM (*/**) 5 mi total	Walk 30 min or XT or off	Speed Day (*/**) 11 x 400	5K easy(2H)	off	Long run 7 mi (12K) xx	off
Week 4						
RR (*/**) 2 mi (15:30) plus 800 meters (1:55 per lap)	Walk 30 min or XT or off	Speed Day 13 x 400 (*/**)	5K easy or XT or off	off	Long run 4 mi (6.5K) xx	off
Week 5						
MM (*/**) 6 mi total	Walk 30 min or XT or off	Speed Day (*/**) 15 x 400	5K easy or XT or off	off	9.5 mi (15K)	off
Week 6						
6 x 400(*/**)	Walk 30 min or XT or off	4 x 400 (*/**)	5K easy or XT or off	off	2.25 mi RR (17:25)	off
Next week: Goal Race						
3-4 x 400 (*/**)	XT or off	3-4 x 400 (*/**)	5K easy or XT or off	off	Goal Race	

TIME GOAL 5K: 28:59

- Wednesday's speed 400 repetitions should be run at 2:12 each

- Long runs should be run no faster than 12 min per mile for quick recovery, adjusting for temperature

- Goal times for Monday's RR time trials are in parentheses

- Total mileage for MM days is listed with "total" at end (MM is embedded in the middle)

- Try to stay smooth at the end of the speed session, even when tired; it's OK to slow down a second or two

Mon	Tues	Wed	Thu	Fri	Sat	Sun
Week 1						
MM (*/**) 4 mi total	Walk 30 min or XT or off	Speed Day (*/**) 7 x 400	5K easy (1H) or XT or off	off	Long run 4 mi (6.5K) xx	off
Week 2						
RR (*/**) 1.5 mi (14:00) plus 1200 meter (2:18 per lap)	Walk 30 min or XT or off	Speed Day 9 x 400 (*/**)	5K easy (2H) or XT or off	off	Long run 5.5 mi (9K) xx	off
Week 3						
MM (*/**) 5 mi total	Walk 30 min or XT or off	Speed Day (*/**) 11 x 400	5K easy (2H) or XT or off	off	Long run 7 mi (12K) xx	off
Week 4						
RR (*/**) 2 mi (18:42) plus 800 meters (2:18 per lap)	Walk 30 min or XT or off	Speed Day 13 x 400 (*/**)	5K easy (1H) or XT or off	off	Long run 4 mi (6.5K) xx	off
Week 5						
MM (*/**) 6 mi total	Walk 30 min or XT or off	Speed Day (*/**) 15 x 400	5K easy or XT or off	off	9.5 mi (15K)	off
Week 6						
6 x 400 (*/**)	Walk 30 min or XT or off (*/**)	4 x 400	5K easy (1H) or XT or off	off	2.25 mi RR (21:03) (*/**)	off
Next week: Goal Race						
3-4 x 400 (*/**)	XT or off	3-4 x 400 (*/**)	5K easy	off	Goal Race	

TIME GOAL 5K: 33:59

- Wednesday's speed 400 repetitions should be run at 2:38 each

- Long runs should be run no faster than 13 min per mile (for quick recovery), adjusting for temperature.

- Goal times for Monday's RR time trials are in parentheses

- Total mileage for MM days is listed with "total" at end (MM is embedded in the middle)

- Try to stay smooth at the end of the speed session, even when tired; it's OK to slow down a second or two

Mon	Tues	Wed	Thu	Fri	Sat	Sun
Week 1						
MM (*/**) 4 mi total	Walk 30 min or XT or off	Speed Day (*/**) 6 x 400	5K easy (1H) or XT or off	off	Long run 4 mi (6.5K) xx	off
Week 2						
RR (*/**) 1.5 mi (16:26) plus 1200 meter (2:43 per lap)	Walk 30 min or XT or off	Speed Day 8 x 400 (*/**)	5K easy (2H) or XT or off	off	Long run 5.5 mi (9K) xx	off
Week 3						
MM (*/**) 5 mi total	Walk 30 min or XT or off	Speed Day (*/**) 10 x 400	XT or off	off	Long run 7 mi (12K) xx	off
Week 4						
RR (*/**) 2 mi (21:54) plus 800 meters (2:43 per lap)	Walk 30 min or XT or off	Speed Day 12 x 400 (*/**)	XT or off	off	Long run 4 mi (6.5K) xx	off
Week 5						
MM (*/**) 6 mi total	Walk 30 min or XT or off	Speed Day (*/**) 14 x 400	XT or off	off	9.5 mi (15K)	off
Week 6						
6 x 400 (*/**)	Walk 30 min or XT or off	4 x 400 (*/**)	XT or off	off	2.25 mi RR (24:40) (*/**)	off
Next week: Goal Race						
3-4 x 400 (*/**)	XT or off	3-4 x 400 (*/**)	off	off	Goal Race	

TIME GOAL 5K: 37:59

- Wednesday's speed 400 repetitions should be run at 2:55 each

- Long runs should be run no faster than 14 min per mile (for quick recovery), adjusting for temperature

- Goal times for Monday's RR time trials are in parentheses

- Total mileage for MM days is listed with "total" at end (MM is embedded in the middle)

- Try to stay smooth at the end of the speed session, even when tired; it's OK to slow down a second or two.

Mon	Tues	Wed	Thu	Fri	Sat	Sun
Week 1						
MM (*/**) 4 mi total	Walk 30 min or XT or off	Speed Day (*/**) 6 x 400	XT or off	off	Long run 4 mi (6.5K) xx	off
Week 2						
RR (*/**) 1.5 mi (18:22) plus 1200 meter (3:00 per lap)	Walk 30 min or XT or off	Speed Day 8 x 400 (*/**)	XT or off	off	Long run 5.5 mi (9K) xx	off
Week 3						
MM (*/**) 5 mi total	Walk 30 min or XT or off	Speed Day (*/**) 10 x 400	XT or off	off	Long run 7 mi (12K) xx	off
Week 4						
RR (*/**) 2 mi (24:30) plus 800 meters (3:00 per lap)	Walk 30 min or XT or off	Speed Day 12 x 400 (*/**)	XT or off	off	Long run 4 mi (6.5K) xx	off
Week 5						
MM (*/**) 6 mi total	Walk 30 min or XT or off	Speed Day (*/**) 14 x 400	XT or off	off	9.5 mi (15K)	off
Week 6						
6 x 400 (*/**)	Walk 30 min or XT or off	4 x 400 (*/**)	XT or off	off	2.25 mi RR (27:36) (*/**)	off
Next week: Goal Race						
3-4 x 400 (*/**)	XT or off	3-4 x 400 (*/**)	off		off	Goal Race

10K SCHEDULES—IF YOU'VE RUN AT LEAST ONE 5K OR 10K

Note: Speedwork increases injury risk. You'll reduce this risk to minimal levels by gradually increasing the number of repetitions, inserting adequate rest, and being sensitive to all "weak link" areas. These are the places that tend to get sore or painful when you run farther or faster than you have been running. When in doubt, don't run as fast, increasing the rest between repetitions and between workouts. If you even suspect that you may have the beginning of an injury, stop the workout immediately.

Symbols: (* = cadence drill) (** = acceleration-glider) See the "Drills" chapter in this book. (xx = run the long run 3:30 min/mi slower than your magic mile predicts in the 10K, adjust for temperature)
(RR = "race rehearsal"; you will be running at goal pace, gradually increasing the distance)

Note: During the RR segments, practice the run-walk-run ratio you plan to use in the race itself.

(MM = "magic mile", which is run in the middle of the running time for that day)
(XT means "cross-training" or alternative exercise such as walking, cycling, swimming, water running)
(H = hill repeats, done on Thursday or Sunday, see segment in primary training components)

TIME GOAL 10K: 34:59

- Wednesday's speed workout of 400 m repetitions should be run at 1:16 each

- Long runs should be run no faster than 9 min/per mile for quick recovery (adjust for temperature)

- If your long run is not up to the distance of the first long run on the schedule, gradually increase to this length before beginning the program

- Goal times for Monday's RR time trials are in parentheses

- Total mileage for MM days is listed with "total" at end (MM is embedded into the middle of the mileage)

- Stay smooth at the end of the speed session, even when tired; it's OK to slow down 1-3 seconds, during the last 2 repetitions for this purpose

Mon	Tues	Wed	Thu	Fri	Sat	Sun
Week 1						
MM (*/**) 4 mi total	Walk 30 min or XT or off	Speed Day (*/**) 8 x 400	5K easy (2H)	off	Long run 8 mi (12.5K) xx	off
Week 2						
RR (*/**) 2.25 mi (12:42) plus 1200 meter (1:22 per lap)	Walk 30 min or XT or off	Speed Day 10 x 400 (*/**)	5K easy (3H)	off	Long run 10 mi (16K) xx	off
Week 3						
MM (*/**) 5 mi total	Walk 30 min or XT or off	Speed Day (*/**) 12 x 400	5K easy	off	Long run 5 mi (8K) (4H)	off

Week 4

| RR (*/**) 2.75 mi (15:30) plus 800 m (1:22 per lap) | Walk 30 min or XT or off | Speed Day 14 x 400 (*/**) | 5K easy (3H) | off | Long run 12.5 mi (20.5K) xx | off |

Week 5

| MM (*/**) 6 mi total | Walk 30 min or XT or off | Speed Day (*/**) 16 x 400 | 5K easy | off | 6 mi (4H) (10K) | off |

Week 6

| RR (*/**) 3.25 mi (18:20) plus 1200 m (1:22 per lap) | Walk 30 min or XT or off | Speed Day 18 x 400 (*/**) | 5K easy (2H) | off | Long run 15 mi (24K) xx | off |

Week 7

| MM (*/**) 5 mi total | Walk 30 min or XT or off | Speed Day (*/**) 20 x 400 | 5K easy | off | 6 mi (4H) (10K) | off |

Week 8

| RR (*/**) 3.75 mi (21:10) plus 800 m (1:22 per lap) | Walk 30 min or XT or off | Speed Day 22 x 400 (*/**) | 5K easy or XT or off | off | Long run 17 mi (28K) xx | off |

Week 9

| 8 x 400 (*/**) | Walk 30 min or XT or off (*/**) | 6 x 400 (*/**) | 5K easy or XT or off | off | 4.25 mi RR (24:00) | off |

Next week: Goal Race

| 5-6 x 400 (*/**) | XT or off | 3-4 x 400 (*/**) | 5K easy | off | Goal Race | |

TIME GOAL 10K: 39:59

- Wednesday's speed workout of 400 repetitions should be run at 1:29 each

- Long runs should be run no faster than 10 min/per mile for quick recovery (adjust for temperature)

- If your long run is not up to the distance of the first long run on the schedule, gradually increase to this length before beginning the program

- Goal times for Monday's RR time trials are in parentheses

- Total mileage for MM days is listed with "total" at end (MM is embedded into the middle of the mileage)

- Stay smooth at the end of the speed session, even when tired; it's OK to slow down 1-3 seconds, during the last 2 repetitions for this purpose

Mon	Tues	Wed	Thu	Fri	Sat	Sun
Week 1						
MM (*/**) 4 mi total	Walk 30 min or XT or off	Speed Day (*/**) 8 x 400	5K easy (2H)	off	Long run 8 mi (12.5K) xx	off
Week 2						
RR (*/**) 2 mi (12:54) plus 1200 meter (1:35 per lap)	Walk 30 min or XT or off	Speed Day 10 x 400 (*/**)	5K easy (3H)	off	Long run 10 mi (16K) xx	off
Week 3						
MM (*/**) 5 mi total	Walk 30 min or XT or off	Speed Day (*/**) 12 x 400	5K easy	off	5 mi (4H) (8K)	off

Week 4

RR (*/**) 2.5 mi (16:08) plus 800 meters (1:35 per lap)	Walk 30 min or XT or off	Speed Day 14 x 400 (*/**)	5K easy (3H)	off	Long run 12 mi (20.5K) xx	off

Week 5

MM (*/**) 6 mi total	Walk 30 min or XT or off	Speed Day (*/**) 16 x 400	5K easy	off	5 mi (4H) (8K)	off

Week 6

RR (*/**) 3 mi (19:21) plus 1200 meter (1:35 per lap)	Walk 30 min or XT or off	Speed Day 18 x 400 (*/**)	5K easy(2H)	off	Long run 14 mi (22.5K) xx	off

Week 7

MM (*/**) 5 mi total	Walk 30 min or XT or off	Speed Day (*/**) 20 x 400	5K easy	off	5mi (4H) (8K) xx	off 5 mi

Week 8

RR (*/**) 3.5 mi (22:35) plus 800 meters (1:35 per lap)	Walk 30 min or XT or off	Speed Day 22 x 400 (*/**)	5K easy or XT or off	off	Long run 16 mi (25.5K) xx	off

Week 9

8 x 400 (*/**)	Walk 30 min or XT or off	6 x 400 (*/**)	5K easy or XT or off	off	4 mi RR (25:48) (*/**)	off

Next week: Goal Race

5-6 x 400 (*/**)	XT or off	3-4 x 400 (*/**)	5K easy	off	Goal Race	

TIME GOAL 10K: 44:59

- Wednesday's speed workout of 400 repetitions should be run at 1:40 each

- Long runs should be run no faster than 11 min/per mile for quick recovery (adjust for temperature)

- If your long run is not up to the distance of the first long run on the schedule, gradually increase to this length before beginning the program

- Goal times for Monday's RR time trials are in parentheses

- Total mileage for MM days is listed with "total" at end (MM is embedded into the middle of the mileage)

- Stay smooth at the end of the speed session, even when tired; it's OK to slow down 1-3 seconds, during the last 2 repetitions for this purpose

Mon	Tues	Wed	Thu	Fri	Sat	Sun
Week 1						
MM (*/**) 4 mi total	Walk 30 min or XT or off	Speed Day (*/**) 8 x 400	5K easy (2H) or XT or off	off	Long run 7 mi (11.5K) xx	off
Week 2						
RR (*/**) 2 mi (14:30) plus 1200 meter (1:46 per lap)	Walk 30 min or XT or off	Speed Day 10 x 400 (*/**)	5K easy (3H) or XT or off	off	Long run 9 mi (14.5K) xx	off
Week 3						
MM (*/**) 5 mi total	Walk 30 min or XT or off	Speed Day (*/**) 12 x 400	5K easy or XT or off	off	5 mi (4H) (8K)	off

Week 4

RR (*/**) 2.5 mi (18:09) plus 800 meters (1:46 per lap)	Walk 30 min or XT or off	Speed Day 14 x 400 (*/**)	5K easy (2H) or XT or off	off	Long run 11 mi (17.5K) xx	off

Week 5

MM (*/**) 6 mi total	Walk 30 min or XT or off	Speed Day (*/**) 16 x 400	5K easy or XT or off	off	5 mi (3H) (8K)	off

Week 6

RR (*/**) 3 mi (21:46) plus 1200 meter (1:46 per lap)	Walk 30 min or XT or off	Speed Day 18 x 400 (*/**)	5K easy or XT or off	off	Long run 13 mi (21K) xx	off

Week 7

MM (*/**) 5 mi total	Walk 30 min or XT or off	Speed Day 20 x 400	5K easy	off	5 mi (3H)	off

Week 8

RR (*/**) 3.5 mi (25:21) plus 800 m (1:46 per lap)	Walk 30 min or XT or off	Speed Day 22 x 400 (*/**)	5K easy or XT or off	off	Long run 15 mi (24K) xx	off

Week 9

8 x 400 (*/**)	Walk 30 min or XT or off	6 x 400 (*/**)	5K easy or XT or off	off	4 mi RR (29:00) (*/**)	off

Next week: Goal Race

5-6 x 400 (*/**)	XT or off	3-4 x 400 (*/**)	5K easy	off	Goal Race

TIME GOAL 10K: 49:59

- Wednesday's speed workout of 400 repetitions should be run at 1:51 each

- Long runs should be run no faster than 12 min/per mile for quick recovery (adjust for temperature)

- If your long run is not up to the distance of the first long run on the schedule, gradually increase to this length before beginning the program

- Goal times for Monday's RR time trials are in parentheses

- Total mileage for MM days is listed with "total" at end (MM is embedded into the middle of the mileage)

- Stay smooth at the end of the speed session, even when tired; it's OK to slow down 1-3 seconds, during the last 2 repetitions for this purpose

Mon	Tues	Wed	Thu	Fri	Sat	Sun
Week 1						
MM (*/**) 4 mi total	Walk 30 min or XT or off	Speed Day (*/**) 6 x 400	5K easy (1H) or XT or off	off	Long run 6 mi (10K) xx	off
Week 2						
RR (*/**) 2 mi (16:07) plus 1200 m (1:59 per lap)	Walk 30 min or XT or off	Speed Day 8 x 400 (*/**)	5K easy (2H) or XT or off	off	Long run 8 mi (13K) xx	off
Week 3						
MM (*/**) 5 mi total	Walk 30 min or XT or off	Speed Day (*/**) 10 x 400	5K easy or XT or off	off	4 mi (3H) (5.6K)	off

Week 4

RR (*/**) 2.5 mi (20:09) plus 800 m (1:59 per lap)	Walk 30 min or XT or off	Speed Day 12 x 400 (*/**)	5K easy (2H) or XT or off	off	Long run 10 mi (16K) xx	off

Week 5

MM (*/**) 6 mi total	Walk 30 min or XT or off	Speed Day (*/**) 14 x 400	5K easy or XT or off	off	5 mi (3H) (8K)	off

Week 6

RR (*/**) 3 mi (24:11) plus 1200 m (1:59 per lap)	Walk 30 min or XT or off	Speed Day 16 x 400 (*/**)	5K easy (1H) or XT or off	off	Long run 12 mi (17.5K) xx	off

Week 7

MM (*/**) 5 mi total	Walk 30 min or XT or off	Speed Day (*/**) 18 x 400	5K easy or XT or off	off	5 mi (3H) (8K)	off

Week 8

RR (*/**) 3.5 mi (28:12) plus 800 meters (1:59 per lap)	Walk 30 min or XT or off	Speed Day 20 x 400 (*/**)	5K easy or XT or off	off	Long run 14 mi (21.5K) xx	off

Week 9

6 x 400 (*/**)	Walk 30 min or XT or off	6 x 400 (*/**)	5K easy or XT or off	off	4 mi RR (32:14) (*/**)	off

Next week: Goal Race

5-6 x 400 (*/**)	XT or off	3-4 x 400 (*/**)	5K easy	off	Goal Race

TIME GOAL 10K: 54:59

- Wednesday's speed workout of 400 repetitions should be run at 2:04 each

- Long runs should be run no faster than 13 min/per mile for quick recovery (adjust for temperature)

- If your long run is not up to the distance of the first long run on the schedule, gradually increase to this length before beginning the program

- Goal times for Monday's RR time trials are in parentheses

- Total mileage for MM days is listed with "total" at end (MM is embedded into the middle of the mileage)

- Stay smooth at the end of the speed session, even when tired; it's OK to slow down 1-3 seconds, during the last 2 repetitions for this purpose

Mon	Tues	Wed	Thu	Fri	Sat	Sun
Week 1						
MM (*/**) 4 mi total	Walk 30 min or XT or off	Speed Day (*/**) 6 x 400	XT or off	off	Long run 6 mi (10K) xx	off
Week 2						
RR (*/**) 2 mi (17:44) plus 1200 meter (2:11 per lap)	Walk 30 min or XT or off	Speed Day 8 x 400 (*/**)	XT or off	off	Long run 8 mi (13K) xx	off
Week 3						
MM (*/**) 5 mi total	Walk 30 min or XT or off	Speed Day (*/**) 10 x 400	XT or off	off	Long run 4 mi (5.6K) xx	off

Week 4

RR (*/**) 2.5 mi (22:09) plus 800 meters (2:11 per lap)	Walk 30 min or XT or off	Speed Day 12 x 400 (*/**)	XT or off	off	Long run 10 mi (16K) xx	off

Week 5

MM (*/**) 6 mi total	Walk 30 min or XT or off	Speed Day (*/**) 14 x 400	XT or off	off	5 mi (8K)	off

Week 6

RR (*/**) 3 mi (26:48) plus 1200 meter (2:11 per lap)	Walk 30 min or XT or off	Speed Day 16 x 400 (*/**)	XT or off	off	Long run 12 mi (17.5K) xx	off

Week 7

MM (*/**) 5 mi total	Walk 30 min or XT or off	Speed Day (*/**) 18 x 400	XT or off	off	Long run 5 mi (8K) xx	off

Week 8

RR (*/**) 3.5 mi (31:03) plus 800 meters (2:11 per lap)	Walk 30 min or XT or off	Speed Day 20 x 400 (*/**)	XT or off	off	Long run 14 mi (21.5K) xx	off

Week 9

4 x 400 (*/**)	Walk 30 min or XT or off	6 x 400 (*/**)	XT or off	off	4 mi RR (35:28)	off

Next week: Goal Race

5-6 x 400 (*/**)	XT or off	3-4 x 400 (*/**)	XT or off	off	Goal Race	

TIME GOAL 10K: 59:59

- Wednesday's speed workout of 400 repetitions should be run at 2:16 each

- Long runs should be run no faster than 14 min/per mile for quick recovery (adjust for temperature)

- If your long run is not up to the distance of the first long run on the schedule, gradually increase to this length before beginning the program

- Goal times for Monday's RR time trials are in parentheses

- Total mileage for MM days is listed with "total" at end (MM is embedded into the middle of the mileage)

- Stay smooth at the end of the speed session, even when tired; it's OK to slow down 1-3 seconds, during the last 2 repetitions for this purpose

Mon	Tues	Wed	Thu	Fri	Sat	Sun
Week 1						
MM (*/**) 4 mi total	Walk 30 min or XT or off	Speed Day (*/**) 6 x 400	XT or off	off	Long run 6 mi (10K) xx	off
Week 2						
RR (*/**) 2 mi (19:20) plus 1200 meter (2:22 per lap)	Walk 30 min or XT or off	Speed Day 8 x 400 (*/**)	XT or off	off	Long run 8 mi (13K) xx	off
Week 3						
MM (*/**) 5 mi total	Walk 30 min or XT or off	Speed Day (*/**) 10 x 400	XT or off	off	Long run 4 mi (5.6K) xx	off

Week 4						
RR (*/**) 2.5 mi (24:11) plus 800 meters (2:22 per lap)	Walk 30 min or XT or off	Speed Day 12 x 400 (*/**)	XT or off	off	Long run 10 mi (16K) xx	off

Week 5						
MM (*/**) 6 mi total	Walk 30 min or XT or off	Speed Day (*/**) 14 x 400	XT or off	off	5 mi (8K)	off

Week 6						
RR (*/**) 3 mi (29:00) plus 1200 meter (2:22 per lap)	Walk 30 min or XT or off	Speed Day 16 x 400 (*/**)	XT or off	off	Long run 12 mi (17.5K) xx	off

Week 7						
MM (*/**) 5 mi total	Walk 30 min or XT or off	Speed Day (*/**) 18 x 400	XT or off	off	Long run 5 mi (8K) xx	off

Week 8						
RR (*/**) 3.5 mi (33:49) plus 800 meters (2:22 per lap)	Walk 30 min or XT or off	Speed Day 20 x 400 (*/**)	XT or off	off	Long run 14 mi (21.5K) xx	off

Week 9						
4 x 400 (*/**)	Walk 30 min or XT or off (*/**)	6 x 400	XT or off	off	4 mi RR (38:42) (*/**)	off

Next week: Goal Race						
5-6 x 400 (*/**)	XT or off	3-4 x 400 (*/**)	XT or off	off	Goal Race	

TIME GOAL 10K: 1:09

- Wednesday's speed workout of 400 repetitions should be run at 2:38 each

- Long runs should be run no faster than 15 min/per mile for quick recovery (adjust for temperature)

- If your long run is not up to the distance of the first long run on the schedule, gradually increase to this length before beginning the program

- Goal times for Monday's RR time trials are in parentheses

- Total mileage for MM days is listed with "total" at end (MM is embedded into the middle of the mileage)

- Stay smooth at the end of the speed session, even when tired; it's OK to slow down 1-3 seconds, during the last 2 repetitions for this purpose

Mon	Tues	Wed	Thu	Fri	Sat	Sun
Week 1						
MM (*/**) 4 mi total	Walk 30 min or XT or off	Speed Day (*/**) 6 x 400	XT or off	off	Long run 6 mi (10K) xx	off
Week 2						
RR (*/**) 2 mi (22:15) plus 1200 meter (2:48 per lap)	Walk 30 min or XT or off	Speed Day 8 x 400 (*/**)	XT or off	off	Long run 8 mi (13K) xx	off
Week 3						
MM (*/**) 5 mi total	Walk 30 min or XT or off	Speed Day (*/**) 10 x 400	XT or off	off	Long run 4 mi (5.6K) xx	off

Week 4

RR (*/**) 2.5 mi (27:48) plus 800 meters (2:48 per lap)	Walk 30 min or XT or off	Speed Day 12 x 400 (*/**)	XT or off	off	Long run 10 mi (16K) xx	off

Week 5

MM (*/**) 6 mi total	Walk 30 min or XT or off	Speed Day (*/**) 14 x 400	XT or off	off	5 mi (8K)	off

Week 6

RR (*/**) 3 mi (33:20) plus 1200 meter (2:48 per lap)	Walk 30 min or XT or off	Speed Day 16 x 400 (*/**)	XT or off	off	Long run 12 mi (17.5K) xx	off

Week 7

MM (*/**) 5 mi total	Walk 30 min or XT or off	Speed Day (*/**) 18 x 400	XT or off	off	Long run 5 mi (8K) xx	off

Week 8

RR (*/**) 3.5 mi (38:55) plus 800 meters (2:48 per lap)	Walk 30 min or XT or off	Speed Day 20 x 400 (*/**)	XT or off	off	Long run 14 mi (21.5K) xx	off

Week 9

4 x 400 (*/**)	Walk 30 min or XT or off (*/**)	6 x 400 (*/**)	XT or off	off	4 mi RR (44:30)	off

Next week: Goal Race

5-6 x 400 (*/**)	XT or off	3-4 x 400 (*/**)	XT or off	off	Goal Race

TIME GOAL 10K: 1:19

- Wednesday's speed workout of 400 repetitions should be run at 3:02 each

- Long runs should be run no faster than 16 min/per mile for quick recovery (adjust for temperature)

- If your long run is not up to the distance of the first long run on the schedule, gradually increase to this length before beginning the program

- Goal times for Monday's RR time trials are in parentheses

- Total mileage for MM days is listed with "total" at end (MM is embedded into the middle of the mileage)

- Stay smooth at the end of the speed session, even when tired; it's OK to slow down 1-3 seconds, during the last 2 repetitions for this purpose

Mon	Tues	Wed	Thu	Fri	Sat	Sun
Week 1						
MM (*/**) 4 mi total	Walk 30 min or XT or off	Speed Day (*/**) 6 x 400	XT or off	off	Long run 6 mi (10K) xx	off
Week 2						
RR (*/**) 2 mi (25:27) plus 1200 meter (3:09 per lap)	Walk 30 min or XT or off	Speed Day 8 x 400 (*/**)	XT or off	off	Long run 8 mi (13K) xx	off
Week 3						
MM (*/**) 5 mi total	Walk 30 min or XT or off	Speed Day (*/**) 10 x 400	XT or off	off	Long run 4 mi (5.6K) xx	off

Week 4

RR (*/**) 2.5 mi (31:50) plus 800 meters (3:09 per lap)	Walk 30 min or XT or off	Speed Day 12 x 400 (*/**)	XT or off	off	Long run 10 mi (16K) xx	off

Week 5

MM (*/**) 6 mi total	Walk 30 min or XT or off	Speed Day (*/**) 14 x 400	XT or off	off	5 mi (8K)	off

Week 6

RR (*/**) 3 mi (38:13) plus 1200 meter (3:09 per lap)	Walk 30 min or XT or off	Speed Day 16 x 400 (*/**)	XT or off	off	Long run 12 mi (17.5K) xx	off

Week 7

MM (*/**) 5 mi total	Walk 30 min or XT or off	Speed Day (*/**) 18 x 400	XT or off	off	Long run 5 mi (8K) xx	off

Week 8

RR (*/**) 3.5 mi (44:35) plus 800 meters (3:09 per lap)	Walk 30 min or XT or off	Speed Day 20 x 400 (*/**)	XT or off	off	Long run 14 mi (21.5K) xx	off

Week 9

4 x 400 (*/**)	Walk 30 min or XT or off	6 x 400 (*/**)	XT or off	off	4 mi RR (50:55) (*/**)	off

Next week: Goal Race

5-6 x 400 (*/**)	XT or off	3-4 x 400 (*/**)	XT or off	off	Goal Race

Chapter 10

WHAT HAPPENS TO US AS WE TRAIN?

THE "TEAM" OF HEART, LUNGS, NERVES, BRAIN, ETC.

Very often, in professional sports, a group of very talented individuals is defeated by a group of players of lesser ability who play as a "team". Each of the training elements on your 5K/10K schedule will help you improve. But when you do them regularly, and blend them into a gradual progression, your overall capacity and performance potential is greater than that produced by the sum of the individual parts.

The heart gets stronger—like any muscle, the heart's strength and effectiveness is increased through regular endurance exercise. Those doing speedwork will coax some extra adaptations out of the cardiovascular system.

The lungs become more efficient in processing oxygen and inserting it into the blood

Endorphins (natural painkillers) reduce discomfort, and give you a relaxing and positive attitude as you push back the threshold of endurance and speed.

The long runs push back your endurance "wall" far beyond race distance. By gradually extending slow long runs, you train muscle cells to expand their capacity to utilize oxygen efficiently, sustain energy production, and in general, increase capacity to go farther. The continued extension of the distance of long runs increases the reach of blood system capillaries to deliver oxygen as it encourages the body to improve the efficiency of the return of waste products. With this improved "plumbing system" the muscles can work at top capacity for a longer distance. These improvements help you keep going at the end: you're tired but strong.

First-time 5K/10K runners will do the minimum on two other days (i.e., Tues and Thurs). A half-hour run on Tuesday and Thursday will maintain the endurance gained on the weekend. Very few injuries occur when runners follow this plan. If you are already running more than this, without aches and pains, you can continue if you wish—but be careful. Time goal runners have speed or hill training on these days.

Drills improve running form and help you run smoother and easier.

Speed training pushes back your anaerobic threshold. With each successive speed session you train yourself to go farther at your goal pace. At the end of each workout you are tired, but you can keep going when running at the right pace for that day. You simulate the conditions that you'll experience at the end of the race as you mold body, mind, and spirit into a team.

Chapter 11

5K & 10K DRILLS
TO MAKE RUNNING FASTER AND EASIER

The following drills have helped thousands of runners prepare for 5K and 10K races. Beginners will find that running is easier when they do the two simple drills each week. Veterans will be able to stay smoother when running at race pace, after they have done a few drills, two days a week. Each targets a few key capabilities. When you put all of them together, they can help you run lighter on your feet, with better form, while strengthening key muscle groups. When runners do these regularly, they tend to eliminate excess motion of feet and legs, reduce impact, reduce the effort of running, and increase the cadence or turnover of your feet and legs. Each drill teaches you to run more directly and efficiently.

WHEN?

These should be done on a non-long-run day. It is fine, however, to do them as part of your warm-up before a MM, race, or a speed workout. Many runners have also told me that the drills are a nice way to break up an average run that they might otherwise call "boring".

CADENCE DRILL ("CD") IMPROVES TURNOVER OF FEET AND LEGS

This easy drill improves running efficiency, while reinforcing the key elements of good running form. Over the weeks and months, if you do this drill once every week, you will find that your normal cadence naturally and slowly increases.

1. Warm up by walking for 5 minutes, and running and walking very gently for 10 minutes.

2. Start jogging slowly for 1-2 minutes, and then time yourself for 30 seconds. During this half-minute, count the number of times your left foot touches the ground.

3. Walk around for a minute or so.

4. On the second 30-second drill, increase the count by 1 or 2.

5. Repeat this 3-7 more times, each time trying to increase by 1-2 additional counts.

6. If you reach a count that you can't exceed—just try to maintain.

In the process of improving turnover, the body's internal monitoring system coordinates a series of adaptations which makes the feet, legs, nerve system, and internal timing mechanism work together as an efficient team:

- Your foot touches more gently, and quicker

- Extra, inefficient motions of the foot and leg are reduced or eliminated

- Less effort is spent on pushing up or moving forward

- You stay lower to the ground

- The ankle becomes more efficient

- Ache and pain areas are not overused

ACCELERATION-GLIDER DRILLS
(NOTED AS "ACG" ON THE TRAINING SCHEDULE)

This drill is a form of speed play, or fartlek. By using it regularly, you develop a range of speeds with the muscle conditioning to move smoothly from one to the next. The greatest benefit comes as you learn how to "glide", or coast off your momentum.

1. Done on a non-long-run day, in the middle of a shorter run, or as a warm-up for a speed session or a race—or test day.

2. Warm up with at least half a mile of easy running.

3. Many runners do the cadence drill just after the easy warm-up, and then do the acceleration-gliders. But you can separate the two drills if you wish.

4. Run 4-8 of them.

5. Do this at least once a week.

6. No sprinting—never run all-out.

After teaching this drill at my one-day running schools and weekend retreats for years, I can say that most people learn better through practice when they work on the concepts listed next (rather than the details) of the drill. So just get out there and try them!

Gliding—The most important concept. Imagine yourself coasting off the momentum of a downhill run—you're gliding. Some of your gliders can be on a downhill slope, if you want. But it is important to do at least two of them on the flat land. Your goal is to use momentum, if only for 5-10 strides.

Do this every week—As in the cadence drills, the regularity of the drill is very important. If you're like most runners, you won't glide very far at first. Weekly practice will teach you to glide farther and farther.

Don't sweat the small stuff—I've included a general guideline for the "step count" for each part of the drill, but don't worry about getting an exact number. It's best to get into a flow with this drill, so that one segment may be longer and another much shorter.

Smooth transition—This should happen between each of the components. Each time you "shift gears" you are using the momentum of the current mode to start you into the next mode. Don't make a sudden and abrupt change, but strive for a smooth transition.

HERE'S HOW IT'S DONE

- Start by jogging very slowly for about 15 steps.

- Then, jog faster for about 15 steps—increasing to a regular running pace for you.

- Now, over the next about 15 steps, gradually increase the speed to your current race pace.

- OK, it's time to glide, or coast. Allow yourself to gradually slow down to a jog using momentum as long as you can. At first you may only glide for 4 or 5 steps. As the months go by you will get up to 20, then 30, and beyond....you're gliding!

Overall purpose—As you do this drill every week, you will feel smoother at each mode of running. Congratulations! You are learning how to keep moving at a fairly fast pace without using much energy. This is the main object of the drill.

Some weeks you'll glide longer than others. By doing this drill regularly, you will find yourself coasting or gliding down the smallest of inclines, and even for 10-20 yards on the flat, on a regular basis. Gliding conserves energy, reduces soreness and fatigue, and maintains a faster pace in races.

Chapter 12

SPEED TRAINING IS CRUCIAL FOR 5K/10K PERFORMANCE

At some point, virtually every runner wants to run a little faster. Often this is due to the envy of others who started when you did, but have recorded faster finish times a year later. Beware! Some very sedentary people inherited a better set of fitness genes. The reality is that the first item most runners desire, when they want to add spice to their running, is a faster pace. This chapter will explain how speed training helps, the pitfalls, and the internal changes that allow you to run faster.

I don't recommend training for a time goal in your first 5K or 10K. After you've finished your first campaign, come back to this chapter. During your first training program, focus on the sense of satisfaction and achievement from pushing back your endurance through the long runs. Success in your first race is crossing the finish line **(in the upright position, hopefully with a smile on your face).**

Learn your limits. Most people go through their lives without ever testing their physical limits or experiencing the enrichment that comes from extending them. Once beginning speed trainers realize that they will be capable of responding to the challenge, some get a little carried away and push too hard in the quest for improvement. The most common speed training mistake is doing too much, too soon. The series of gentle increases in the training schedules in this book will gradually extend your capacity to go farther—at a slightly faster pace than you are running now. Since each person can control the effort level, you can always maintain control by being more conservative. The improvement process involves guessing and adjusting, going just a bit farther, and then backing off. When done regularly, speed training helps mind, body, and spirit work as a team as you blend all of the body systems for improvement.

Each workout will provide a slight increase in the number of speed repetitions. At the same time that you improve muscle conditioning and cardiovascular performance, you'll gain pace judgment and mental toughness. The overall experience of doing this, even for one season, progressively reduces the anxiety of race day. Pushing through a series of gentle doubts can significantly improve confidence in confronting unknown challenges in other areas of life. The only way I've found to prepare for pushing beyond the point of fatigue in races is to simulate the conditions during speed workouts.

Beware of the ego. Some of the most timid beginning runners become overly aggressive competitors. As the times in races improve through regular training, the ego says to push even more. "If I improved 10 seconds with one weekly speed workout, then two hard workouts will double the improvement."

In this way, speed-trained runners mistakenly allow egos to equate running satisfaction with time improvement or age group placing. An ego-driven runner loses the joy in finishing and the glow of endorphins because the watch says that he or she didn't achieve some arbitrary standard. This line of thinking often leads to slower races (due to overtraining) and disappointment. Using an analogy of a piece of cake, I suggest that you enjoy the texture and flavor of the cake itself (the vitality and mental attitude boost from a run), and appreciate any time improvement as a tasty icing on top.

It is healthy to let your ego have its moments of glory, as you perform well. Just realize that improvement is not a continuous upward journey, and the ego has a problem with any downturn. A natural selection process occurs during a speed training season, as the ego is forced to deal with reality and make adjustments. But by maintaining the enjoyment of a fun run every week, running with friends, and appreciating the afterglow from any run, you can maintain a balanced set of rewards, while keeping the ego in check.

Due primarily to weather and other factors outside your control, be prepared to record times which are slower than you think you should be running on at least half of your races. This is often due to the ego telling you to run faster than your current ability or present conditions. Be patient, learn from your setbacks, and you will generally move forward.

So take the leap of faith, and jump into the testing process. By pushing the limits you may learn more about yourself than in any other activity in life. The real treasure is ahead: finding hidden strengths that can help you deal with even greater challenges in races and in life itself.

GETTING FASTER REQUIRES EXTRA WORK

To get faster, you must push beyond your current performance capacity. Be careful! Even a small amount over your speed limit can result in longer recovery or injury. The secret is to push only a little harder on each workout, then rest enough so the systems can rebound and improve. Gradual and gentle increases are always better because you are more likely to sustain continuous and long-term improvement.

Our bodies are programmed to conserve resources by doing the smallest amount of work they can get away with. So even after we have increased the length of our runs, steadily over several months, our leg muscles, tendons, ligaments, etc. are not prepared for the jolt that speed training delivers. The best way to stay injury free is to start with a few speed repetitions and gradually increase the duration and intensity. But only when we take enough rest between the speed workouts can the body rebuild and improve performance capability.

- Mitochondria (energy powerhouses inside muscle cell) increase capacity and output
- Mechanical efficiency of the foot is improved—more work done with less effort
- Legs go farther when tired—adaptations allow you to keep going
- Muscle cells work as a team—getting stronger, increasing performance, pumping blood back to heart
- Mental concentration increases
- Your spirit is unleashed as you find yourself improving

ENDORPHINS KILL PAIN AND MAKE YOU FEEL GOOD

Running at any pace, but especially speed training, signals to your body that there will be some pain to kill. The natural response is to produce internal pain killers called endorphins. These hormones act as drugs that relax and deal with muscle discomfort, while bestowing a good attitude—especially when you are tired after the run. Walking during the rest interval allows the endorphins to collect—so you'll feel even better.

GRADUALLY PUSHING UP THE WORKLOAD

Your body is programmed to improve when it is gradually introduced to a little more work with enough rest afterward. Push too hard, or neglect the rest, and you'll see an increase in aches, pains, and injury. When speed workouts are balanced, adjustments are made to problems, and goals are realistic, most runners can continue to improve for years.

SPEED "REPETITIONS" AND REST "INTERVALS"

Speed workouts are set up with repetitions of segments (usually laps around a track) followed by a rest interval for recovery. When we run a little faster than our realistic goal pace, and increase the number of repetitions a little more than we did on last week's speed workout, this greater workload breaks down the muscle cells, tendons, etc. and stimulates change. You see, our bodies are programmed to rebuild, stronger than before, when slightly overwhelmed. But there must be gentle and regular stress, followed by significant rest to promote this regeneration.

INTRODUCING THE BODY TO SPEED THROUGH DRILLS

As a gentle introduction to faster running, I've found nothing better than the two drills that are detailed in the "Drills" chapter: Cadence Drills & Acceleration-Gliders. The former helps to improve cadence of the legs and feet. The latter provides a very gentle introduction to speedwork in very short segments. Most of the running during the conditioning period is at an easy pace. These drills, done in the middle of a short run, once or twice a week, will improve mechanics, get the muscles ready for the heavier demands of speed training, and initiate internal physiological changes in the muscles—with very little risk of injury.

A GENTLE INCREASE IN YOUR WEEKLY WORKOUTS CAUSES A SLIGHT BREAKDOWN

The weekly speed workout starts with a few speed repetitions, with rest between each. As the number of repetitions increase each week your body is pushed slightly beyond what it did the previous week. In each workout, your muscle fibers get tired as they reach the previous maximum workload, and continue like motivated slaves to keep you running at the pace assigned. In every session some are pushed beyond their capacity with each additional speed repetition. Often, pain and fatigue are not felt during the workout. But within one or two days you'll experience sore muscles and tendons and general overall tiredness. Even walking may not feel smooth for a day or two after a speed session that is run too hard. A few of these symptoms is fine. When you have a lot of them—you did too much. Too much work tends to result in a negative attitude also.

THE DAMAGE

Looking inside the cell at the end of a hard workout, you'll see damage:

- Tears in the muscle cell membrane

- The mitochondria (that process the energy inside the cell) are swollen

- There's a significant lowering of the muscle stores of glycogen (the energy supply needed in speedwork)

- Waste products from exertion, bits of bone, and muscle tissue and other bio junk can be found

- Sometimes, there are small tears in the blood vessels and arteries, and blood leaks into the muscles

THE DAMAGE STIMULATES THE MUSCLES, TENDONS, ETC. TO REBUILD STRONGER AND BETTER THAN BEFORE

Your body is programmed to get better when it is pushed beyond its current limits. A slight increase is better than a greater increase because the repair can be done relatively quickly.

YOU MUST HAVE ENOUGH REST IF YOU WANT TO REBUILD STRONGER AND BETTER

Two days after a speed session, if the muscles have had enough rest, you'll see some improvements:

- Waste has been removed

- Thicker cell membranes can handle more work without breaking down

- The mitochondria have increased in size and number, so that they can process more energy next time

- The damage to the blood system has been repaired

- Over several months, after adapting to a continued series of small increases, more capillaries (tiny fingers of the blood system) are produced; this improves and expands the delivery of oxygen and nutrients and provides a better withdrawal of waste products

These are only some of the performance components that improve capacity: biomechanics, nervous system, strength, muscle efficiency, and more. Internal psychological improvements follow the physical ones. Mind, body, and spirit are becoming a team, improving health and performance. An added benefit is a positive attitude.

QUALITY REST IS CRUCIAL: 48 HOURS BETWEEN WORKOUTS

On rest days, it's important to avoid exercises that strenuously use the calf muscle, ankle, and achilles tendon (stair machines, step aerobics, spinning out of the saddle) for the 48-hour period between running workouts. If you have other aches and pains from your individual "weak links" then don't do exercises that aggravate them. Walking is usually a great exercise for a rest day. There are several other good exercises in the "Cross-training" section of this book. As long as you are not continuing to stress the calf, most alternative exercises are fine.

BEWARE OF JUNK MILES

Those training for a time goal often develop injuries because they try to "sneak in" a few miles on the days they should be resting. Even more than running long distance, speed training stresses the feet and legs and mandates the need for a 48-hour recovery period. The short, junk mile days don't help your conditioning, but they keep your muscles from recovering.

REGULARITY

To maintain the adaptations, you must regularly run about every two days. To maintain the speed improvements mentioned in this book, you should do the speed work listed in the training schedules, about every week (acceleration-gliders and cadence drills) and the speed repetitions. It is OK to delay a workout every once in a while, but you need to stay on the schedule as close as possible. Missing two workouts in a row will result in a slight loss in the capacity you have been developing. The longer you wait, the harder it will be to start up again.

"MUSCLE MEMORY"

Your neuromuscular system remembers the patterns of muscle activity which you have done regularly over an extended period of time. The longer you have been running regularly, the more easily it will be to start up when you've had a layoff. During your first few months of speedwork, for example, if you miss a weekly workout, you will need to drop back a week, and rebuild. But if you have run regularly for several years, and you miss a speed workout, little will be lost if you start the next one very slowly, and ease into it. Be careful as you return to speed training, if this happens.

TIP: CRAMPED FOR TIME? JUST DO A FEW REPETITIONS

Let's say that you cannot get to the track on your speed day, and you don't have but 15 minutes to run. Take a 3-4 minute slow warm-up with some accelerations, and do the same, in reverse, during the last 3-5 minutes. During the middle 5-9 minutes, run several 1-2 minute acceleration-gliders at approximately the pace you would run on the track. Don't worry if the pace is not perfect. Any of these segments is better than a week without any fast running at all. Then, the following week, you can do the workout (or most of it) that had been planned for that week.

AEROBIC RUNNING IS DONE DURING LONG RUNS

Aerobic means "in the presence of oxygen". This is the type of running you do when you feel "slow" and comfortable. When running aerobically, your muscles can get enough oxygen from the blood to process the energy in the cells (burning fat in most cases). The minimal waste products produced during aerobic running can be easily removed, with no lingering build up in the muscles.

SPEED TRAINING GETS YOU INTO THE ANAEROBIC ZONE: CREATING AN OXYGEN DEBT

Anaerobic running involves going too fast or too long for you on that day. At some point in the workout, when you reach your current limit, the muscles can't get enough oxygen to burn the most efficient fuel, fat. So they shift to the limited supply of stored sugar: glycogen. The waste products from this fuel pile up quickly in the cells, tightening the muscles and causing you to breathe heavily. You have encountered a condition called an "oxygen debt". If you keep running for too long in this anaerobic state, you will have to slow down significantly or stop. But if you are running for a realistic time goal, and are pacing yourself correctly, you should only be running anaerobically for a short period of time, at the end of each workout and race.

THE ANAEROBIC THRESHOLD

As you increase the quantity of your speed sessions, you push back your anaerobic threshold. This means that you can run a bit farther than before—each week, at the same pace, without extreme huffing and puffing. Your muscles can move your body farther and faster without going to exhaustion. Each speed workout pushes you a little bit further into the anaerobic zone. Speedwork trains the body and mind to go farther before going anaerobic, how to deal with the discomfort this produces, and how to keep going when the muscles are tight and tired. It also tells you that you don't have to give up on performance when in this state. The process of coping with the stress of speedwork is the essence of running faster.

THE TALK TEST: HOW AEROBIC ARE YOU?

- You're aerobic—if you can talk for as long as you want with minimal huffing & puffing (h & p)

- You are mostly aerobic—if you can talk for 30 sec + then must h & p for no more than 10 sec

- You are approaching anaerobic threshold—if you can only talk for 10 seconds or less, then h & p for 10+ sec

- You're anaerobic—if you can't talk more than a few words, and are mostly h + p

ARE YOU WORKING TOO HARD TOWARD A TIME GOAL?

When runners get too focused on specific time goals they often feel more stress and experience some negative attitude changes. At the first sign of these symptoms, back off and let mind and body get back together again.

- Running is not as enjoyable

- You don't look forward to your runs

- When you say something to others about your running, the statements are often negative

- The negativity can permeate other areas of your life

- You look on running as work instead of play

THE PERSONAL GROWTH OF SPEED TRAINING

Instead of looking just at the times in your races, embrace the life lessons that can come from the journey of enhancing your overall physical performance and endurance. The unexpected fun in most of your runs will help you through the challenges. Even after a hard workout, focus on how good you feel afterward, and the satisfaction from overcoming adversity.

The reality of a speed training program is that you'll have more setbacks than victories. But you will learn more from the setbacks, they will make you a stronger runner—and you will develop inner strength. Confronting challenges is initially tough, but leads you to some of the great treasures of the improvement process. As you dig for deeper resources you find that you have more strength inside than you thought.

Chapter 13

5K/10K RACE DAY TIMETABLE

Most runners who arrive at their first 5K or 10K are surprised at the upbeat atmosphere. If the energy could be put in a container, and used in your car, you wouldn't have to buy fuel for weeks. Almost everyone at a race is in a good mood, and the shared excitement and optimism of the start continues through the after-race party.

WHAT TO LOOK FOR IN A RACE

- Fun and festive

- Good refreshments afterward

- T-shirt and other goodies

- Entertainment

- If this is your first race, look for one that has a lot of fun elements, food, and a high percentage of first-time racers

- If you're trying to improve your finish time, pick one that is not too crowded, has a good reputation for organization and a course that is not to difficult (avoid hills, lots of turns, etc.)

OTHER FACTORS TO CONSIDER

- Difficulty of the course—ask your resources (next section) about this. Pick a course that tends to produce fast times.

- Weather conditions—look at the average temperatures for the day on which the race is scheduled to be held. Ideal temperature is below 60°F (14°C). Remember that for every 5 degrees above 60°F (2°C above 14°C), you will tend to slow down by 30 sec a mile 20 sec/kilometer.

- Well organized—the organizers...keep things organized: accurate measurement, accurate timing (usually using "the chip" technology), no long lines, easy to register, start goes off on time, water on the course, refreshments for all—even the slowest, no major problems.

- Competitive runners like the event and respect the organizers.

RESOURCES: WHERE TO FIND OUT ABOUT RACES

Running stores

This resource is at the top of our list because you can usually get entry forms plus some editorial comment about the race. Explain to the store folks that this is your first race, or that you're going for a fast time. Select a fun event that has a high rating in the previous "what to look for" section.

Friends who run

Call a friend who has run for several years. Tell him or her that you are looking for a fun, upbeat race. Go over the same categories listed previously. Be sure to ask the friend for a contact number or website where you can find more information on the event, and possibly enter. As with running store staff, the editorial comments and evaluation of an event can steer you to a good experience.

Running clubs

If there is a running club or two in your area, get in touch. The officers or members can recommend several events. Running clubs may be found by doing a web search: type "running clubs (your town)". The RRCA (Road Runner's Club of America) is a national organization of neighborhood clubs. From their website, search for a club in your area.

Newspaper listings

In many newspapers, there is a listing of community sports events in the weekend section. This comes out on Friday or Saturday in most cities, usually in the lifestyle section. Some listings can be in the sports section under "running" or "road races".

Web Searches

A web search for "road races (your town)" or "5K (your town)" is often productive. There are several event companies that serve as a registration center for many races: including www.active.com and www.marathonguide.com. From these sites you can sometimes find an event in your area, research it, and then sign up.

HOW TO REGISTER

1. Online. More and more of the road running events are conducting registration online. This allows you to bypass the process of finding an entry form, and sending it in before the deadline.

2. Fill out an entry and send it in. Entry forms are found in running stores, health clubs, etc. You will need to fill out your name, address, T-shirt size, etc., and then sign the waiver form. Be sure to include a check for the entry fee.

3. Show up on race day. Because some races don't do race day registration, be sure that you can do this. There is usually a penalty for waiting until the last minute—but you can see what the weather is like before you make the trek to the race.

Rehearsal

If at all possible, run one or more of your long runs on the race course. You'll learn how to get there, where to park (or which rapid transit station to exit), and what the site is like. If you will be driving, drive into the parking area several times to make sure you understand how to go exactly where you need to park. This will help you to feel at home with the staging area on race day. Run over the last half mile of the course at least twice. This is the most important part of the course to know. It's also beneficial to do the first part of the course to see which side of the road is best for walk breaks (sidewalks, etc.)

Visualize your lineup position. First-time racers should line up at the back. If you are too far forward, you could slow down runners that are faster. You want to do this first race slowly, and have a good experience. This is most likely at the back of the pack. Because you will be taking your walk breaks, as in training, you need to stay at the side of the road. If there is sidewalk, you can use this for your walk breaks.

THE AFTERNOON BEFORE

Don't run the day before the race. You won't lose any conditioning if you take two days off from exercise before the race. Some races have "expos", one to three days before. Companies in the running business have displays, shoes, clothing, books, etc.—often at sale prices. Beware of sale shoes, however. It is best to go to a good running store and go through the procedure noted in the shoe chapter to select a shoe that is designed for the type of foot that you have.

Some races require you to pick up your race number, and sometimes your computer chip the day before. Look at the website or the entry form for instructions about this. Most races allow you to pick up your materials on race day—but be sure.

Race number

This is sometimes called a "bib number". It should be pinned on the front of the garment you'll be wearing when you cross the finish line.

Computer chip

More and more races are using technology that electronically picks up your race number and time as you cross the finish. You must wear this chip that is usually laced on the shoes, near the top. Some races provide you with a velcro band that holds the chip to the ankle or arm. Read the instructions to make sure you are attaching this correctly. Some races include the chip as part of the bib. Be sure to turn this in after the race. Officials have volunteers to collect them, so stop and take them off your shoe, etc. There is a steep fine for those who don't turn in the chip.

The carbo-loading dinner

Some races have a dinner the night before. At the dinner you will usually chat with runners at your table, and enjoy the evening. Don't eat much, however. Many runners assume, mistakenly, that they must eat a lot of food the night before. This is actually counterproductive. It takes at least 24 hours for most of the food you eat to be processed and useable in a race—usually longer. Assume that there is nothing you can eat the evening before a race that will help you.

A lot of food in your gut, when you are bouncing up and down in a race, is stressful. A very common and embarrassing situation occurs when the gut is emptied to relieve this stress. While you don't want to starve yourself the afternoon and evening before, the best strategy is to eat small meals, and taper down the amount as you get closer to bed time. As always, it's best to have done a "rehearsal" of eating, so that you know what works, how much, when to stop eating, and what foods to avoid. The evening before your long run is a good time to work on your eating plan. Adjust and replicate the successful routine leading to race day.

Drinking

The day before, drink regularly. If you haven't had a drink of water or sports drink in a couple of hours, drink about 8 oz (about 250 ml) each hour. Don't drink a lot of fluid during the 60-90 minutes before the race. This can lead to bathroom breaks during the race itself. Many races have porto-johns around the course, but some do not. It is a very common practice for runners that have consumed too much fluid that morning to find a tree or ally along the course. A common practice is to drink 6-10 oz of fluid about 2 hours before the race. Usually this is totally out of the system before the start.

> **TIP**
>
> If you practice drinking before your long runs, you can find the right amount of fluid that works best for you on race day. Stage your drinks so that you know when you will be taking potty breaks.

THE NIGHT BEFORE

Eating is optional after 6pm. If you are hungry, have a light snack that you have tested before, and has not caused problems. Less is better, but don't go to bed hungry. Continue to have about 8 oz of a good electrolyte beverage like Accelerade over the 2 hours before you go to bed.

Alcohol is not generally recommended because the effects of this central nervous system depressant carry over to the next morning. Some runners have no trouble having one glass of wine or beer, while others are better off with none. If you decide to have a drink, I suggest that you make it one portion.

Pack your bag and lay out your clothes so that you don't have to think very much on race morning.

- Your watch, set up for the run-walk ratio you are using
- Shoes
- Socks
- Shorts
- Top—see clothing thermometer
- Pin race # on the front of the garment in which you will be finishing
- A few extra safety pins
- Water, Accelerade, pre-race and post-race beverages (such as Endurox R4), and a cooler if you wish
- Food for the drive in and the drive home
- Bandages, vasoline, any other first aid items you may need
- Cash for registration if you are doing race day registration (check for exact amount, including late fee)

- $ 25-40 for gas, food, parking, etc.
- Race chip attached according to the race instructions
- A few jokes or stories to provide laughs or entertainment before the start
- A copy of the "race day checklist", which follows

Sleep

You may sleep well, or you may not. Don't worry about it if you don't sleep at all. Many runners I work with every year don't sleep at all the night before and have the best race of their lives. Of course, don't try to go sleepless....but if it happens, it is not a problem.

Race day checklist

Photocopy this list so that you will not only have a plan, you can carry it out in a methodical way. Pack the list in your race bag. Don't try anything new the day of your race—except for health or safety. The only item I have heard about when used for the first time in a race that has helped is walk breaks. Even first time users benefit significantly. Otherwise, stick with your plan.

Fluid and potty stops—after you wake up, drink the amount of water you have found manageable before long runs. If you have used Accelerade about 30 minutes before your runs, prepare it. Use a cooler if you wish. In order to avoid the bathroom stops, stop your fluid intake according to what has worked for you before. Don't try any new fluid on race day.

Eat—what you have eaten before your harder runs. It is OK not to eat at all before a 5K or 10K unless you are a diabetic (or have other needs), then go with the plan that you and your doctor (or nutritionist) have worked out.

Get your bearings—walk around the site to find where you want to line up (at the back of the pack, or in a pace group), and how you will get to the start. Choose a side of the road that has more shoulder or sidewalk for ease in taking walk breaks.

Register or pick up your race number—if you already have all of your materials, you can bypass this step. If not, look at the signage in the registration area and get in the right line. Usually there is one for "race day registration" and one for those who registered online or in the mail and need to pick up their numbers.

Start your warm up 40-50 min before the start. If possible, go backwards on the course for about .5-.6 mi and turn around. This will give you a preview of the most important part of your race—the finish. Here is the warm-up routine:

- Walk for 5 minutes, slowly

- Walk at a normal walking pace for 3-5 minutes, with a relaxed and short stride

- Start your watch for the ratio of running and walking that you are using and do this for 10 minutes.

- Walk around for 5-10 minutes

- If you are shooting for a time goal, do a few acceleration-gliders: 4-8 of them

- If you have time, walk around the staging area, read your jokes, laugh, relax

- Get in position and pick one side of the road or the other where you want to line up

- When the road is closed, and runners are called onto the road, go to the curb and stay at the side of the road, near or at the back of the crowd (for first-timers)

AFTER THE START

Remember that you can control how you feel during and afterward by conservative pacing and walks.

- Stick with the run/walk ratio that has worked for you—take every walk break, especially the first one

- If it is warm, slow down and walk more (30 sec/mi slower for each 5°F above 60°F/20sec/km for each 2°C above 14°C)

- Don't let yourself be pulled out too fast on the running portions

- As people pass you, who don't take walk breaks, tell yourself that you will catch them later—you will!

- If anyone interprets your walking as weakness, say: "This is my proven strategy for a strong finish"

- Talk with folks along the way, enjoy the course, smile often

- On warm days, pour water over your head at the water stops (no need to drink on a 5K unless you want to)

AT THE FINISH

- In the upright position

- With a smile on your face

- Wanting to do it again

AFTER THE FINISH

- Keep walking for at least half a mile

- Drink about 4-8 oz of fluid

- Within 30 min of the finish, have a snack that is 80% carbohydrate/20% protein (Endurox R4 is best)

- If you can soak your legs in cool water, during the first two hours after the race, do so for 10-20 min

- Walk for 20-30 minutes later in the day

THE NEXT DAY

- Walk for 30-60 minutes, very easy; this can be done at one time, or in installments

- Keep drinking about 4-6 oz an hour of water or a sports drink like Accelerade

- Wait at least a week before you either schedule your next race or vow to never run another one again

Chapter 14

A JOURNAL GIVES YOU CONTROL OVER YOUR TRAINING

It would be wonderful if we never had to write anything down. But in our daily lives, we tend to remember only a few of the crucial ingredients that help us improve our fitness. Without a journal, you'll probably forget the few small mistakes that led to an injury or the fine-tuning of minor elements that led to a personal record.

A journal allows us to plan the future, track our behaviors, learn from our mistakes, and chart our progress in a consistent direction. With a simple logbook format that each of us chooses, we can see what to do, usually within a few minutes, and make the adjustments necessary. Journals give us control over our future while they allow us to learn from our past.

I'm not suggesting that everything be scheduled in advance. Some of the most inspiring moments and memorable actions sneak up on us unexpectedly. In your journal you can trap these and relive the positive feelings. But by using your journal to plan ahead, you're programming the brain to continuously steer toward interesting opportunities that arise, as you eliminate junk miles and aches. You don't even have to have a time goal to benefit from a journal. Journals are extremely helpful in ensuring that you schedule and record the enjoyable components while avoiding the stressful trends that produce injury.

Of all the activities that surround running, it is the writing and review of your journal that gives the greatest control as you adjust. It only takes a few minutes, every other day, to record the key information. Looking back through your entries will provide laughs and enjoyment. You'll revisit the interesting things you saw during the last week, the crazy thoughts, the people you met and the fun. This process can inspire the right brain to produce more entertainment, as you schedule runs that are more likely to promote the joy of running.

5K/10K JOURNAL KEEPERS ARE MORE LIKELY TO BE LIFELONG RUNNERS OR WALKERS

Many beginners tell me that the writing of each day's mileage in the journal was their greatest motivation—simple but satisfying. After a few weeks, most experience the empowerment earned from organizing workouts in the journal. By the time 6 months have passed, you'll look ahead several months to schedule races, the training needed to prepare for them, and the fun events along the way. I hear from several runners every month who use their journal as a diary of their lives, noting the kid's soccer scores, and PTA notes.

A journal allows you to focus on your day. As you set aside time for your run, you'll find yourself taking more runs per year. The journal is the steering wheel that keeps you on the road to running enjoyment and improvement. As you hold tight and use this "wheel", you control the process.

A SIMPLE REWARD CAN PULL YOU OUT OF THE DUMPS

We all feel better and enjoy our activities when we feel rewarded. The simple act of recording the distance you cover each day will give you a genuine sense of accomplishment that is felt internally. When you string together a series of runs, or walks, on days you didn't feel like exercising, you feel so good inside. Even the most upbeat people have periods of low motivation, and have told me that their journals got them refocused on the down days.

THIS IS YOUR BOOK

Yes, you are writing a book. At the most basic level, you will outline your running life during the next few months. No one tells you what goes into this book. As runners record their entries in the log, they realize that they can use the same journal to organize other areas of life. Even runners who are not fired up about the process at first are usually impressed at how many benefits flow from this tool. Since you don't need to show anyone your journal, you can let your feelings go as you write. Upon review, your emotional response to a given workout can be very interesting months or years later.

CAN YOU CAPTURE THE FLEETING THOUGHTS OF THE RIGHT BRAIN?

One of the interesting challenges and great rewards of journaling is noting the creative and sometime crazy images that emerge from the right side of our head. On some days you won't get any of these, and on others...the faucet opens up. Often the thoughts come out of nowhere. Other times, you will be suddenly hit with a solution to a problem you've been working on for months. If you have your journal available at the place where you return from your run, car, office desk, kitchen countertop, you can quickly jot some key words to describe the images or craziness.

THE VARIOUS TYPES OF JOURNALS

Calendar—facing you on the wall

Many runners start recording their runs on a wall calendar—or one that is posted on the refrigerator. Looking at the miles recorded is empowering. But equally motivating for many is seeing too many "zeros" on days that should have been running days. If you're not sure whether you will really get into this journal process, you may find it easiest to start with a calendar.

An organized running journal

When you use a product that is designed for running, you don't have to think to record the facts. The spaces on the page ask you for certain info, and you will learn to fill in the information very quickly. This leaves you time to use some of the open space for the creative thoughts and ideas that pop out during a run. Look at the various journals available and pick one that looks to be easy to use.

Week of | Jan 1

Thursday
Jan 4

GOAL	35 min easy
	(SC)
TIME	45 min
DISTANCE	@ 6.5
AM PULSE	49
WEATHER	Cloudy
TEMP	40°
TIME	6 AM/PM
TERRAIN	rolling
DATE	WALK BREAK —

1
2
3
4
5
6
7
⑧
9
10

COMMENTS

Great run with Barb, Wes + Sambo — who took out the pace too fast + died at the end. The rest of us caught up on the gossip. Achilles ached so I iced it for 15 minutes.

Friday
Jan 5

GOAL	45 min (sp)
	5 X 800 meter
TIME	1:15
DISTANCE	7.5 mi
AM PULSE	53
WEATHER	45°
TEMP	Sunny
TIME	5 AM/PM
TERRAIN	track
DATE	WALK BREAK 400m

1
2
3
4
⑤ felt
6
7 Perform.
⑧
9
10

COMMENTS

2:30
2:36
2:33
2:37
2:32
2:36

My best workout in years!
- walked 400m between each
- struggled on last one
Achilles ached – iced 15 min
12min warm up and warm down

Saturday
Jan 6

GOAL	Off
TIME	
DISTANCE	
AM PULSE	55
WEATHER	
TEMP	
TIME	AM/PM
TERRAIN	
DATE	WALK BREAK

1
2
3
4
5
6
7
8
9
10

COMMENTS

Kids soccer (Morn)
* Westin scores goal bouncing off his back
1st goal of season!
Brennan's cross country (aft) Invitational
* Brennan comes from 8th to 3rd in the last half mile. I'm so proud!

Sunday
Jan 7

GOAL	18 mi (1)
	easy!
TIME	2:53
DISTANCE	18mi
AM PULSE	52
WEATHER	50°
TEMP	dry no wind
TIME	9 AM/PM
TERRAIN	flat
DATE	WALK BREAK 1min/mi

1
2
3
4
5
⑥
7
8
9
10

COMMENTS

It was great to cover 18 miles — wish I had a group
longest run in 18 months!
but...
* went too fast in the first 5 miles
* Achilles hurt afterward – take 3 days off
* Power Bar + water from 10mi kept spirits up

* Pulse is up – I'm not recovering – need more days off/week

Notebook

You don't need a commercial product. You can use a school notebook, of your choice. Find one of the size that works best with your lifestyle (briefcase, purse, etc.). Following you will find the items that I've found helpful for most runners. The non-limiting nature of a notebook is a more comfortable format for runners that like to write a lot one day, and not so much another day.

Computer and smartphone logs

There are a growing number of software products and smartphone apps that allow you to sort through information more quickly. In working with a company (PC Coach) to incorporate my training program, I discovered that this format speeds up the search for information you need. As you set up your own codes and sections you can pick data that is important to you, sort it to see trends, and plan ahead. Some software (including mine) allows for you to download data from a heart monitor or GPS watch.

THE WRITING PROCESS

1. Capturing the flow from the right brain.
   Try to have the log handy so that you can record info after a run. Jot down the fresh perceptions quickly, before they fade.

2. Just the facts.
   At first, spend a few seconds and quickly record key info. If you have to think about an item skip it and just fill in the items you can. Here's my suggested list:

Date:

Morning pulse:

Time of run:

Distance covered:

Time running:

Weather:

Temp:

Precipitation:

Humidity:

Comments:

Run-Walk-Run frequency:

Any special segments of the run (speed, hills, race, etc.):

Running companion:

Terrain:

How did you feel (1-10):

3. Go back over the list again and fill in more details—emotional responses, changes in energy or blood sugar level, and location of places where you had aches and pains— even if they went away during the run. You are looking for patterns of items that could indicate injury, blood sugar problems, lingering fatigue, etc.

4. Helpful additions (usually in a blank section at the bottom of the page).

   • Improvement thoughts

   • Things I should have done differently

   • Interesting happenings

   • Funny things

   • Strange things

   • Stories, right brain crazy thoughts

ARE YOU TIRED...OR JUST LAZY? YOUR MORNING PULSE MAY TELL

Many people say that they are too tired to run. But after interviewing many who make this claim, I've come to believe that most of the reasons for this sensation is laziness (most will admit this), or low blood sugar. One of the best indicators of real fatigue is your resting pulse, taken in the morning. Your journal can track this (although some runners use a piece of graph paper). My journal has a graph inside.

RECORDING MORNING PULSE

1. As soon as you are conscious—but before you have thought much about anything—count your pulse rate for a minute. Record it before you forget it. If you don't have your journal by your bed, then keep a piece of paper and a pen handy.

2. It is natural for there to be some fluctuations, based upon the time you wake up, how long you have been awake, etc. But after several weeks and months, these will balance themselves out. The ideal would be to catch the pulse at the instant that you are awake, before the shock of an alarm clock, thoughts of work stress, etc.

3. After 2 weeks or so of readings, you can establish a base line morning pulse. Take out the top 2 high readings and then compute an average.

4. The average is your guide. If the rate is 5% higher than your average, take an easy day. When the rate is 10% higher, and there is no reason for this (you woke up from an exciting dream, medication, infection, etc.) then your muscles may be tired indeed. Take the day off if you have a run scheduled for that day.

5. If your pulse stays high for more than a week, call your doctor to see if there is a reason for this (medication, infection, hormones, metabolic changes, etc.).

5K/10K RUNNING FORM

I believe that running is an inertia activity: your mission is simply to maintain momentum. Very little strength is needed to run. The first few strides get you into motion, and your focus thereafter is to stay in motion. To reduce fatigue, aches, and pains, your body intuitively fine-tunes your motion so that you minimize effort, as you continue to move forward with very little effort.

Humans have many biomechanical adaptations for running and walking, which allow us to move forward efficiently. The anatomical origin of movement efficiency, going back a million years, is the combination of the calf muscle, ankle, and the achilles tendon. This is an extremely sophisticated system of levers, springs, balancing devices, and more— involving dozens of component parts amazingly well coordinated. Bio mechanics experts believe that this degree of development was not needed for walking. When our ancient ancestors had to run to survive, the evolution reached a new level of performance.

When we have the right balance of walking and running, very little effort from the calf muscle produces a smooth continuation of forward movement. As the calf muscle gets in better shape, and improves endurance, you can keep going, mile after mile, with little perceived effort. Other muscle groups offer support and fine-tune the process. When you feel aches and pains that might be due to the way you run, going back to the minimal use of the ankle and achilles tendon can often leave you feeling smooth and efficient very quickly.

A BETTER WAY OF RUNNING?

There may be a better way to run for you, one that will leave your legs with more strength and result in fewer aches and pains. The fact is, however, that most runners are not far from great efficiency. Repeated research on runners has shown that most are running very close to their ideal. I believe this is due to the action of the right brain. After tens of thousands of steps, it keeps searching for (and then refines) the most efficient pattern of feet, legs, and body alignment.

In my full day running schools and weekend retreats I conduct an individual running form analysis with runners. After having analyzed over ten thousand runners, I've also found that most are running in a very efficient way. The problems are seldom big ones—but a series of small mistakes. By making a few minor adjustments, most runners can feel better on every run.

THE BIG THREE: POSTURE, STRIDE, AND BOUNCE

In these consultations, I've also discovered that when runners have problems, they tend to occur in three areas: posture, stride, and bounce. And the problems tend to be individual in nature. They occur most often in specific body parts (weak links), because of specific motions. Fatigue increases the irritation of the "weak link" areas. A slight overstride, for example, increases fatigue and then produces a feeling of weakness at the end of a run. As a tired body "wobbles", other muscle groups try to keep the body on course, but are not designed for this.

THREE NEGATIVE RESULTS OF INEFFICIENT FORM

1. Fatigue becomes so severe that it takes much longer to recover.

2. Muscles are pushed so far beyond their limits that they break down and become injured.

3. The experience is so negative, that the desire to run is reduced, producing burnout.

Almost everyone has some slight problem. I don't suggest that everyone should try to create perfect form. But when you become aware of your form problems, and make changes to keep them from producing aches and pains, you'll experience fewer aches, smoother and easier running, and faster times. This chapter can help you understand why aches and pains tend to come out of form problems—and how you may be able to reduce or eliminate them.

YOUR OWN FORM CHECK

In some of my clinics, I use a digital camera that gives instant feedback. If you have one of these cameras, have a friend take pictures of you running, from the side (not running toward or away from the camera) while you run on a flat surface.

IF YOU FEEL RELAXED AND RUNNING IS EASY EVEN AT THE END OF A RUN—YOU'RE PROBABLY RUNNING CORRECTLY

Overall, the running motion should feel easy. There should be no tension in your neck, back, shoulders, or legs. A good way to correct problems is to change posture, foot or leg placement, etc., so that running is easier and there is no tightness or pain.

POSTURE

Good running posture is actually good body posture. The head should be naturally balanced over the shoulders, which are aligned over the hips. As the foot comes underneath, all of these elements are in harmony so that little or no energy is needed to prop up the body.

Forward lean

Posture errors tend to be mostly due to a forward lean—especially when we are tired. The head wants to get to the finish as soon as possible, but the legs can't go any faster. A forward lean will often concentrate fatigue, soreness, and tightness in the lower back or neck.

It all starts with the head. When the head is naturally balanced above the shoulders, the neck muscles can relax. But when there is tension in the neck, or soreness afterward, the head is usually leaning too far forward. This triggers a more general upper body imbalance in which the head and chest are suspended slightly ahead of the hips and feet. Ask a running companion to tell you if and when your head is too far forward, or leaning down. The ideal position of the head is mostly upright, with your eyes focused about 30-40 yards ahead of you.

Sitting back

When the hips get out of alignment, the butt seems to be "sitting back" when observed from the side. This occurs when the pelvis is shifted back. In this position, the legs can't go through a natural range of motion, causing an unnatural shortening of the stride, and more effort needed to run at any pace. Many runners tend to hit harder on their heels when their hips are in this position.

A backward lean is rare

It is rare for runners to lean back, but it happens. In my experience, this is usually due to a structural problem in the spine or hips. If you lean back, and you're having pain in the neck, back, or hips, you should see an orthopedist.

Correction: "Puppet on a string"

The best correction I've found to postural problems has been this mental visualization: imagine that you are a puppet on a string. Suspended from above like a puppet (from the head and each side of the shoulders) your head lines up with the shoulders, the hips come directly underneath, and the feet naturally touch lightly. It won't hurt anyone to do the "puppet" several times during a run.

It helps to combine this image with a deep breath. About every 4-5 minutes, as you start to run after a walk break, take a deep, lower lung breath, straighten up, and say "I'm a puppet". Then imagine that you don't have to spend energy maintaining this upright posture, because the strings attached from above keep you on track. As you continue to do this, you reinforce good posture, as you produce a good "habit".

Upright posture not only allows you to stay relaxed, but it may improve your stride length. When you lean forward, you're cutting your stride to stay balanced. When you straighten up, you'll receive a stride bonus of an inch or so, without any increase in energy. Note: don't try to increase stride length. If it happens by a posture improvement, it will occur naturally.

An oxygen dividend

Breathing improves when you straighten up. A leaning body can't get ideal use out of the lower lungs. This can cause side pain. When you run upright, the lower lungs can receive adequate air, absorb oxygen better, reducing the chance of side pain.

FEET LOW TO THE GROUND

The most efficient stride is a shuffle—with feet low to the ground. As long as you pick your foot up enough to avoid stumbling over a rock or uneven pavement, stay low to the ground. Most runners don't need more than 1-inch clearance.

Your ankle combined with your achilles tendon will act as a spring, moving you forward on each running step. If you stay low to the ground, very little effort is required. Through this "shuffling" technique, running becomes almost automatic. When runners err on bounce, they try to push off too hard. This usually results in extra effort spent to lift the body off the ground. You can think of this as energy wasted in the air—energy that could be used to run another mile or two.

There is also a gravity penalty from bouncing too much. The higher you rise, the harder you will fall. Each additional bounce off the ground delivers a lot more impact on feet and legs. This significantly increases aches, pains, and injuries on long runs.

The correction for too much bounce: Light touch

The ideal foot placement should be a landing so light that you don't usually feel any foot impact. This means that your foot stays low to the ground and goes though an efficient and natural motion. Instead of trying to overcome gravity, you get in synch with it.

Here's a "light touch drill": During the middle of a run, time yourself for 20 seconds. Focus on one item: touching so softly that you don't hear your feet. Earplugs are not allowed for this drill. Imagine that you are running on thin ice or through a bed of hot coals. Do several of these 20 second touches, becoming quieter and quieter.

STRIDE LENGTH

Studies have shown that as runners get faster, the stride length shortens. This clearly shows that the key to faster and more efficient running is increased cadence or turnover of feet and legs.

A major cause of aches, pains, and injuries is a stride length that is too long. At the end of this chapter you'll see a list of problems and how to correct them. When in doubt, it is always better to err on the side of having a shorter stride.

Don't lift your knees!

Even world class distance runners don't do this, because even a slight lifting of the upper legs will increase the fatigue of the quadracep muscle (front of the thigh). This often results in a stride that is too long to be efficient. If you suffer from sore quads after a long run or race, you may be lifting the legs too high during the last mile or so.

Don't kick out too far in front of you!

The natural movement of the leg allows the foot to kick forward slightly before it comes back and touches the ground. Let this be a natural motion that produces no tightness in the muscles behind the lower or upper leg. The knee should be slightly bent as you absorb body weight.

Tightness in the front of the shin, or behind the knee, or in the hamstring (back of the thigh) is a sign that you are kicking too far forward. Correct this by staying low to the ground, shortening the stride, and lightly touching the ground.

HILL RUNNING FORM

- Start with a comfortable stride—fairly short

- As you go up the hill, shorten the stride

- Touch lightly with your feet

- Maintain a body posture that is perpendicular to the horizontal (upright, not leaning forward or back)

- Pick up the turnover of your feet as you go up and over the top

- Keep adjusting stride so that the leg muscles don't tighten up—you want them as resilient as possible

- Relax as you go over the top of the hill, and glide (or coast) a bit on the downside

HILL TRAINING STRENGTHENS LOWER LEGS AND IMPROVES RUNNING FORM

The incline of the hill forces your legs to work harder as you go up. The extra work up the incline and the faster turnover, builds strength. By taking an easy walk between the hills, and an easy day afterward, the lower leg muscles become stronger. Over several months, the improved strength allows you to support your body weight farther forward on your feet. An extended range of motion of the ankle and achilles tendon results in a "bonus" extension of the foot forward—with no increase in effort. You will run faster without working harder. What a deal!

RUNNING FASTER ON HILLS IN RACES

Once you train yourself to run with efficient hill form, you'll run faster with increased turnover on the hill workouts. This prepares you to do the same in races. You won't run quite as fast in a race as in your workouts. But through hill training you can run faster than you used to run up the same hill on a race course.

Hill technique during a race follows this pattern: keep shortening stride as you move up the hill. Monitor your respiration rate: don't huff and puff more than you were doing on the flat terrain. As runners improve hill technique in races, they find that a shorter and quicker stride reduces effort while increasing speed—with no significant increase in breathing rate.

Note: On your long runs and easy running days, just jog up hills; don't try to run faster. If respiration rate increases on a hill, reduce stride length until you're breathing as on flat land.

DOWNHILL FORM

- Run light on your feet

- Maintain an average stride—avoid the temptation to extend stride

- Keep feet low to the ground

- Let gravity pull you down the hill

- Turnover of the feet will pick up

- Try to glide (or coast) quickly down the hill

- You shouldn't have to use your quad muscles (front of thigh) when you use this technique

BIGGEST MISTAKES: TOO LONG A STRIDE, BOUNCING TOO MUCH

Even when one or two inches too long, your downhill speed can get out of control. If you are bouncing more than an inch or two off the ground you run the risk of pounding your feet, having to use your quads to slow down (producing soreness), and creating hamstring soreness due to overstride. Best indicator of overstride is tight hamstrings (big muscle behind your upper leg).

Chapter 16

WALKING FORM AND "SHUFFLING"

Most people walk correctly when they use a gentle and comfortable walking motion. But every year, there are walkers who get injured because they are walking in a way that aggravates some area of the foot or leg. Most of these problems come from trying to walk too fast, with too long a stride, or from using a race walk or power walk technique (which I don't recommend).

1. Avoid a long walking stride. Maintain a relaxed motion that does not stress the knees, tendons, or muscles of the leg, feet, knees, or hips. If you feel pain or aggravation in these areas, shorten stride. Many walkers find that they can walk fairly fast with a short stride. When in doubt, walk more slowly and gently.

2. Don't lead with your arms. Minimal arm swing is best. Swinging the arms too much can encourage a longer walk stride which can result in aches and pains. The extra rotation of knees, hips, etc., can lead to longer recovery or injury. The legs should set the rhythm for your walk, allowing you to get into a delightful pattern of right brain thoughts that some call "the zone".

3. Let your feet move the way that is natural for them. When walkers try unnatural techniques that supposedly increase stride length by landing farther back on the heel or pushing farther on the toe, than the legs are designed to move, many get injured. I don't recommend race walking or power walking for this reason.

4. Walking sticks? Many long distance walkers have enjoyed using this European import, which gives the hands and arms "something to do". These adapted ski poles have hand grips that are molded to the human hand for secure gripping. On tough terrain, they may aid in balance. On flat terrain the poles lightly touch the ground. When pesky dogs appear, you have a means of defense. In races, however, they may trip up other walkers or runners.

"SHUFFLING" CAN REDUCE FATIGUE, SORENESS, ACHES

Shuffling is barely moving your feet and legs, to let the walking muscles recover. Most of the time you're doing it right if you feel comfortable, aren't huffing and puffing, and don't have any aches or pains after your first 10 minutes of walking. You are the captain of your walking ship and it is you who determines how far, how fast, how much you will walk, etc. If you choose to insert shuffle breaks from the beginning of any walk that is long for you, you will gain a major degree of control over fatigue, aches, and pains.

WHAT IS A "SHUFFLE"?

With your feet next to the ground, use a short stride with minimal movement. You're still moving forward, but not having to spend much energy doing so. When you insert 30-60 seconds of shuffling into a regular walk, every 2-4 minutes, your walking muscles relax and rest. This lowers the chance of aches and pains due to the constant use of the muscles, tendons, etc.

SHUFFLE BEFORE YOU GET TIRED

Most of us, even when untrained, can walk for several miles before fatigue sets in, because walking is an activity that we are bioengineered to do for hours. Many beginners get discouraged, however, because during the first session or two they don't feel that they are going as far as they should—and add a mile or two. During the mileage extension, they often feel strong, and hardly tired. In a day or two they know otherwise as overused muscles complain.

The continuous use of the walking muscles and tendons—even when the walking pace feels completely comfortable—increases stress on our "weak links", increasing aches and pains much more quickly. If you shuffle before your walking muscles start to get tired, you tend to recover instantly. This increases your capacity for exercise while reducing the chance of a next-day soreness attack.

A STRATEGY THAT GIVES YOU CONTROL

You can't wait until you're tired—you must insert the "shuffles" from the beginning. In setting up a conservative strategy of walk/shuffle, you gain control over fatigue, soreness, and aches. Using this fatigue-reduction tool early gives you muscle strength and mental confidence to the end. Even when you don't need the extra muscle strength and resiliency bestowed by the method, you will feel better during and after your walk, and will finish knowing that you could have gone further, while recovering faster.

Shuffle breaks allow you a chance to enjoy every walk. By taking them early and often you can feel strong, even after covering a distance that is very long for you. There is no need be exhausted at the end of a walk, if you insert enough shuffle breaks, for you, on that day.

A SHORT AND VERY GENTLE SHUFFLE

During the shuffle you are only slightly moving your feet and legs. This allows the tendons, muscles, etc. to recover from your regular walking motion. Keep the feet next to the ground, taking baby steps, barely moving the legs.

NO NEED TO EVER ELIMINATE THE SHUFFLE BREAKS

Some beginners assume that they must work toward the day when they don't have to take any shuffle breaks at all. This is up to the individual, but is not recommended. Remember that you decide what ratio of walk-shuffle to use. I suggest that you adjust the ratio to how you feel on a given day.

Even the most experienced walker has a few "weak links" that are irritated from continuous use. Shuffling can manage these—or eliminate them.

HOW TO KEEP TRACK OF THE SHUFFLE BREAKS

There are several watches which can be set to beep when it's time to shuffle, and then beep again when it's time to walk. Check my website (www.jeffgalloway.com) or a good running store for advice in this area.

HOW TO USE SHUFFLE BREAKS

1. Beginners could walk for 2 minutes and shuffle for 30 seconds. If you feel good during and after the walk, continue with this ratio. If not, adjust the ratio until you feel good.

2. Shuffle breaks allow the body to warm up more easily. If your legs feel tight or you have some soreness, walk for a minute and shuffle for 20-30 seconds—for the first 10 minutes. As the legs loosen up, reduce the shuffles as necessary.

3. On walks longer than 45 minutes, even experienced walkers find that a 30-second shuffle, after about 4 minutes of walking, helps recovery, and reduces aches and pains.

4. On any given day, when you need more shuffling, do so. Don't ever be afraid to drop back to make the walk more fun, and less tiring.

Chapter 17

LOWERING BODY FAT: LESS PAVEMENT POUNDING, FASTER TIMES, QUICKER RECOVERY

With less fat on your body, you will feel bette and can run/walk faster. It is possible to burn fat while training for a 5K or 10K, but you need to ensure that you're recovering well from the long runs (and speed sessions if you are doing these). The concepts in this chapter can help you add to the fat-burning, while you train for your goal. But don't try to lose too much weight at one time.

10,000 MORE STEPS A DAY

A pedometer, or step counter, can help you become a fat-burner—all day long. This device gives you incentive and reinforcement for adding extra steps to your day. It also gives you a sense of control over your actual calorie burnoff. Once you get into the practice of taking more than 10,000 steps a day in your everyday activities, you'll find yourself getting out of your chair more often, parking farther away from the supermarket, walking around the kid's playground, practice field, etc.

30-70 POUNDS OF FAT....GONE

Depending upon how many times you do the following each week, you have many opportunities each day to burn a little here, and a little there. These are easy movements that don't produce tiredness, aches, or pains, but at the end of the year, it really adds up:

Pounds per year	Activity
1-2 pounds	taking the stairs instead of the elevator
10-30 pounds	getting out of your chair at work to walk down the hall
5-10 pounds	getting off the couch to move around the house (but not to get potato chips)
1-2 pounds	parking farther away from the supermarket, mall, etc.
1-3 pounds	parking farther away from your work
2-4 pounds	walking around the kids playground, practice field (chasing the kids)
2-4 pounds	walking up and down the concourse as you wait for your next flight
3-9 pounds	walking the dog each day
2-4 pounds	walking a couple of times around the block after supper
2-4 pounds	walking a couple of times around the block during lunch hour at work
2-4 pounds	walking an extra loop around the mall, supermarket, etc. to look for bargains (this last one could be expensive when at the mall)
Total: More than 30-70 pounds a year	

WEBSITES AND APPS TELL YOU CALORIE BALANCE AND NUTRIENT BALANCE

The best tool I've found for managing your food intake is a good website or software program. There are a number of these that will help you keep your calorie scale balanced (calories burned vs calories eaten). Most of these will have you log in your exercise and what you eat for the day. At the end of the day, you can retrieve an accounting of calories and of nutrients. If you are low on certain vitamins or minerals, protein, etc., after dinner, you can eat food or a vitamin pill the next day. Some programs will tell vegetarians whether they have received enough complete protein, since this nutrient is harder to put together from vegetable sources. If you ate too many calories, you can walk after dinner or increase your step count the next day. For information on current websites, visit www. JeffGalloway.com. It helps to try several before choosing one.

EATING EVERY 2 HOURS—8-10 POUNDS LIGHTER IN A YEAR

If you have not eaten for about 3 hours, your body senses that it is going into a starvation mode, reducing the metabolism rate, while increasing the production of fat-depositing enzymes. This means that you will not be burning as many calories as is normal, that you won't be as mentally and physically alert, and that more of your next meal will be stored away as fat.

If the starvation reflex starts working after 3 hours, then you can beat it by eating every 2 hours. This is a great way to burn more calories. A person who now eats small meals 2-3 times a day can burn about 8-10 pounds a year more when he or she shifts to eating 8-10 times a day. This assumes that the same number of calories are eaten every day.

MOTIVATION INCREASES WHEN YOU EAT MORE OFTEN

The most common reason I've found for low motivation in the afternoon is not eating regularly enough during the day—especially during the afternoon. If you have not eaten for 4 hours or more, and you're scheduled for a workout that afternoon, you will not feel very motivated because of low blood sugar and low metabolism. Even when you've had a bad eating day, and feel "down in the dumps", a snack (such as a fibrous energy bar with a cup of coffee, tea, or diet drink) can reverse the negative mindset. But you don't have to get yourself into this situation if you eat every 2-3 hours.

SATISFACTION FROM A SMALL MEAL—TO AVOID OVEREATING

The number of calories you eat per day can be reduced if you choose combinations of foods that leave you satisfied longer. Sugar is the worst problem in calorie control and satisfaction. Your mission is to find the right combination of foods in your small meals that will leave you satisfied for 2-3 hours. Then, eat another snack that will do the same. You will find a growing number of food combinations that probably have fewer calories, but keep you from getting hungry until your next snack.

FAT + PROTEIN + COMPLEX CARBS = SATISFACTION

Eating a snack that has a variety of the three satisfaction ingredients fat, protein, and complex carbs, will lengthen the time that you'll feel satisfied—even after some small meals. These three items take longer to digest, and therefore keep the metabolism rate revved up.

RECOMMENDED PERCENTAGES OF THE THREE NUTRIENTS:

There are differing opinions on this issue. Here are the ranges given by a number of top nutritionists that I have read and interviewed. These are listed as a percentage computed by dividing the calories consumed in each nutrient by the total number of calories per day.

Protein: between 20% and 30%
Fat: between 15% and 25%
Carbohydrate: whatever is left—hopefully in complex carbohydrates

THE BLOOD SUGAR LEVEL (BSL) DETERMINES HOW GOOD YOU FEEL

When it is at a good, stable level you have enough energy to do what you need to do. If you eat too much sugar, your BSL can rise too high. You'll feel

really good for a while, but the excess sugar triggers a release of insulin. This usually causes a lowering of the BSL—to an uncomfortable level. In this state you don't have energy, mental focus is foggy, and motivation drops.

By managing your BSL throughout the day, you'll be more motivated to exercise, and add other movement to your life. This results in a positive mental attitude, better stress management, and improved problem solving. Eating throughout the day can maintain stable blood sugar, and bestow a feeling of well-being.

DO I HAVE TO EAT BEFORE RUNNING?

Only if your blood sugar is low (or you're diabetic) should you eat before the start. Most who run/walk in the morning don't need to eat anything beforehand. As mentioned, if your blood sugar level is low in the afternoon, and you have a run scheduled, a snack can help. A fibrous energy bar, for example, and a cup of coffee can work wonders when taken about 30 minutes before the run. If you feel that a morning snack will help, the only issue is to avoid consuming so much that you get an upset stomach.

For best results in raising blood sugar when it is too low (within 30 minutes before a run), a snack should have about 80% of the calories in simple carbohydrate and 20% in protein. This promotes the production of insulin which is helpful in this specific case (immediately before a run) in getting the glycogen in your muscles ready for use. The product Accelerade has worked best among the thousands of runners I hear from every year. It has the 80%/20% ratio of carb to protein. If you eat an energy bar with the 80/20 ratio, be sure to drink 6-8 oz of water with it.

PRACTICAL EATING ISSUES

- You don't need to eat before a workout, unless your blood sugar is low (see the previous chapter), or you have an individual need to eat before exercise.

- Reload most effectively by eating within 30 minutes of the finish (80 carb/20 protein)

- Eating or drinking too much right before the start can interfere with deep breathing and may cause side pain. The food or fluid in your stomach limits the intake of air into the lower lungs and restricts the action of the diaphragm.

- If you are running low on blood sugar at the end of your long ones, take some blood sugar booster with you (see the previous chapter for suggestions).

- It is never a good idea to eat a huge meal. Those who claim that they must "carbo load", with a large meal the night before, are rationalizing their desire to eat a lot of food. Eating a big meal the night before (or the day of) a long run can be a real problem. You will have a lot of food in your gut, and you will be bouncing up and down for an extended period. This can lead to an ugly outcome.

EATING DURING EXERCISE

Most exercisers don't need to worry about eating or drinking during a run until the length exceeds 90 minutes. At this point, there are several options. In this case, most runners wait until the 30-40 minute mark in the workout before starting to take the blood sugar booster. Diabetics may need to eat sooner and more often—but this is an individual issue.

GU or Gel products—These come in small packets, and are the consistency of honey or thick syrup. The most successful way to take them is to put 1-3 packets in a small plastic bottle with a pop-top. About every 10-15 minutes, take one or two squirts with a sip or two of water.

Energy Bars—Cut into 8-10 pieces and take 1-2 pieces, with a couple of sips of water, every 10-15 minutes.

Candy—particularly gummi bears or hard candies. The usual consumption is 1-3 about every 10 minutes.

Sports Drinks—Since I've seen a significant increase of nausea among those who drink these products during exercise, I recommend water as the race beverage. If you have found that you can tolerate a certain product during long runs, use it exactly as you have used it before. A sports drink like Accelerade is helpful the day before or after a strenuous run. During a run, I recommend water.

IT IS IMPORTANT TO RELOAD WITHIN 30 MINUTES AFTER EXERCISE

Whenever you have finished a hard or long workout (for you), a recovery snack will help you bounce back faster. Again, the 80/20 ratio of carb to protein has been most successful in reloading the muscles. The product that has worked best among the thousands I work with each year is Endurox R4.

MOST IMPORTANT NUTRIENT: WATER

Whether you choose water, juice, or other fluids, drink regularly throughout the day. Under normal circumstances, your thirst is a good guide for fluid consumption. However, after the age of about 40, this mechanism breaks down. In general, 8 cups of water, per day, is enough for most people (about 1900 ml per day).

Having to take bathroom stops during walks or runs generally means that you are drinking too much—either before or during the exercise. During an exercise session of 60 minutes or less, most exercisers don't need to drink at all. The intake of fluid before exercise should be arranged so that the excess fluid is eliminated before the run. Each person is a bit different, so you will have to find a routine that works for you. Most find that by drinking fluid 60 minutes or more before the start, the potty stop(s) can be made before the start.

Even during extremely long runs/walks of over 4 hours, medical experts from major marathons recommend no more than 27 oz (800 ml) of fluid in an hour, and most drink far less than this amount.

SWEAT THE ELECTROLYTES

Electrolytes are the ions in the salts that your body loses when you sweat: sodium, potassium, magnesium, and calcium. When these minerals get too low, your fluid transfer system doesn't work as well and you may experience ineffective cooling, swelling of the hands, and other problems. Most runners have no problem replacing these in a normal diet. But if you're experiencing cramping regularly during or after exercise, you may be low in sodium or potassium. The best product I've found for replacing these minerals is called SUCCEED. If you have high blood pressure (or any issue with electrolytes), get your doctor's guidance before taking any salt supplement.

When you are sweating a lot, it is a good idea to drink several glasses a day of a good electrolyte beverage. Accelerade is the best I've seen for both maintaining fluid levels and electrolyte levels.

RUN/WALK EATING SCHEDULE

- 1 hour before a morning run: either a cup of coffee or a glass of water Hint: I carry with me little packets of coffee concentrate and can have a cup of coffee quickly. Caffeine, when taken about an hour before exercise, engages the systems that enhance running and extend endurance.

- 30 min before any run (if blood sugar is low) about 100 calories of Acclerade.

- Within 30 min after a run: about 200 calories of a 80% carb/20% protein product (Endurox R4, for example).

- If you are sweating a lot during hot weather, 3-4 glasses of a good electrolyte beverage like Accelerade, when not running, at various times of the day.

MEAL IDEAS

Breakfast Options

1. Whole-grain bread made into french toast with fruit yogurt, juice, or frozen juice concentrate as syrup

2. Whole-grain pancakes with fruit and yogurt

3. A bowl of Grape Nuts Cereal, skim milk, non-fat yogurt, and fruit

4. Smoothie with fiber, fruit, juice, yogurt, etc.

Lunch Options

1. Tuna fish sandwich, whole-grain bread, a little low fat mayo, cole slaw (with fat-free dressing)

2. Turkey breast sandwich with salad, low-fat cheese, celery, and carrots

3. Veggie burger on whole-grain bread, low-fat mayo, salad of choice

4. Spinach salad with peanuts, sunflower seeds, almonds, low-fat cheese, non-fat dressing, whole-grain rolls, or croutons

Dinner Options

There are lots of great recipes in publications such as COOKING LIGHT. The basics are listed here. What makes the meal come alive are the seasonings which are listed in the recipes. You can use a variety of fat substitutes.

1. Fish or lean chicken breast or tofu (or other protein source) with whole wheat pasta, and steamed vegetables

2. Rice with vegetables, and a protein source

3. Dinner salad with lots of different vegetables, nuts, lean cheese or turkey, or fish or chicken

I recommend Nancy Clark's books. Her Sports Nutrition Guidebook is a classic.

Chapter 19

STAYING MOTIVATED

- Consistency is the most important part of conditioning and fitness
- Motivation is the most important factor in being consistent
- You can gain control over your motivation—every day

The choice is yours. You can take control over your attitude, or you can let yourself be swayed by outside factors that will leave you on a motivational roller coaster: fired up one day, with no desire the next. Getting motivated on a given day can sometimes be as simple as saying a few key words and getting out the door. But staying motivated usually requires a strategy or motivational training program. To understand the process, we must first look inside your head.

DISCONNECT BETWEEN THE LEFT BRAIN AND THE RIGHT BRAIN

The brain has two hemispheres that are separated and don't interconnect. The logical left brain does our business activities, trying to steer us into pleasure and away from discomfort. The creative and intuitive right side is an unlimited source of solutions to problems and connections to hidden strengths.

Stress activates the negative left brain. As we accumulate stress, the left brain sends us a stream of logical messages that tell us "slow down", "stop and you'll feel better", "this isn't your day", and even philosophical messages like "why are you doing this". We are all capable of staying on track and maintaining motivation even when the left brain is saying these things.

Take control through mental drills. So the first important step in taking command over motivation is to ignore the left brain unless there is a legitimate reason of health or safety (very rare). You can deal with the left brain through a series of mental training drills. These drills allow the right side of the brain to work on solutions to the problems you are having. As the negative messages spew out of the left brain, the right brain doesn't argue. By using the following information you are preparing for the challenges ahead, while empowering yourself to deal with the problems, as you become mentally tough. But even more important, you will teach yourself three strategies for success.

MAGIC WORDS

Even the most motivated person has segments of a tough workout when he or she wants to quit. By using a successful brainwashing technique, you can pull yourself through these negative thoughts, and feel confident at the end. On these days you have not only reached the finish line—you've overcome challenges to get there.

Each of us has characteristic problems that challenge us. Go back in your memory bank and pull out instances when you started to lose motivation due to one of these, but finished and overcame that challenge.

RELAX.......POWER......GLIDE

During the really tough runs, I have three reoccuring situations: 1) I become tense when I get really tired, worried that I will struggle badly at the end. 2) I feel the loss of the bounce and strength I had at the beginning, and worry that there will be no strength at the end. 3) My form starts to get ragged and I worry about further deterioration of muscles and tendons and more fatigue due to "wobbling".

Over the past three decades I have learned to counter these three problems with the magic words: "Relax...Power....Glide". The visualization of each of these positives helps a little. The real magic comes from the association I have made with hundreds of situations when I started to "lose it" in one of the three areas, but overcame the problems. Each time I overcome one or more of them, I associate the experience with these magic words and add to the magic.

Now, when something starts to go wrong, I repeat the three words, over and over. Instead of increasing my anxiety, I get calm. Even though I don't feel as strong at 5 miles as I did in the first one, I'm empowered just by knowing that I can draw upon my past experience. And when my legs lose the efficient path and bounce, I make adjustments and keep going.

To be successful, you only need to finish the run. Most of the time you can get through the "bad parts" by not giving up, and simply putting one foot in front of the other. As you push beyond the negative left brain messages you develop confidence to do this again, and again. Feel free to use my magic words, or develop your own.

DRILLS

Dirty tricks

The strategy of the rehearsal drill will get you focused, organized, while reducing stress for the first few miles. Magic words will pull you through most of the challenging sessions. But on the really rough days, it helps to have some dirty tricks to play on the left side of the brain.

These are quick fixes that distract the left brain for a while, allowing you to get down the road for a half mile or so. These imaginative and sometimes crazy images don't have to have any logic behind them. But when you counter a left brain message with a creative idea, you have a window of opportunity to get closer to the end of the run.

The giant invisible rubber band

When I get tired on long or hard runs, I unpack this secret weapon, and throw it around someone ahead of me. For a while, the person doesn't realize that he or she has been "looped" and continues to push onward while I get the benefit of being pulled along. After visualizing aspects of this concept for a while, I have to laugh at myself for believing in such an absurd notion. But laughing activates the creative right side of the brain. This usually generates several more entertaining ideas, especially when doing this on a regular basis.

The right brain has millions of dirty tricks. Once you activate it, you're likely to experience solutions to problems you are currently having. It can entertain you as you get another 400-800 yards closer to your finish.

For many more dirty tricks and mental strategies, see GALLOWAY'S BOOK ON RUNNING and HALF-MARATHON: YOU CAN DO IT.

Chapter 20

CROSS-TRAINING FOR THE 5K/10K

My run-walk-run method has helped tens of thousands of new runners avoid injury, while enjoying the increased vitality and attitude that comes with regular running. A growing percentage of these new runners have had such a good experience with running injury free that they think they are immune to aches and pains. They are wrong. Instead of running 2 or 3 days in a row, many runners have eliminated injuries by cross-training every other day.

CROSS-TRAINING ACTIVITIES

The middle ground is to run one day, and cross-train the next. Cross-training simply means "alternative exercise" to running. Your goal is to find exercises that give you the same type of boost as you receive from running, but without tiring the workhorses of running: calf muscles, achilles tendon, ankle, foot.

The other exercises may not deliver the same good feelings—but they can come close. Many runners report that it may take a combination of 3 or 4 different ones in a session. But even if you don't feel exactly the same way, you'll receive the relaxation that comes from exercise, while burning calories and fat.

When you are starting to do any exercise (or starting after a layoff):

1. Start with 5 easy minutes of each exercise, rest for 20 or more minutes, and do 5 more easy minutes.

2. You may do 3-5 different exercises during a cross-training session if they don't use the same muscles.

3. Take a day of rest after this type of exercise (you can do another exercise the next day).

4. Increase by 2-3 additional minutes on each exercise, each session until you get to the number of minutes desired.

5. Once you have reached two 15-minute workouts, you could shift to one 22-25 minute session and increase by 2-3 more minutes per session if you wish.

6. It's best to do no exercise the day before a long run.

7. To maintain your conditioning in each exercise it's best to do one session a week of 10 minutes or more once your reach that amount.

8. The maximum cross-training is up to the individual. As long as you are feeling fine for the rest of the day and having no trouble with your runs, the length of your cross-training should not be a problem.

WATER RUNNING CAN IMPROVE YOUR RUNNING FORM

All of us have little flips and side motions of our legs that interfere with our running efficiency. The resistance of the water forces your legs to find a more efficient path. In addition, several leg muscles are strengthened which can help your legs to keep moving when they get tired at the end of a long run.

HERE'S HOW!

You'll need a flotation belt for this exercise. The product "aqua jogger" is designed to float you off the bottom of the pool, and on most runners, tightens so that it is close to the body. There are many other ways to keep you floating, including simple ski float belts and life jackets.

Get in the deep end of the pool and move your legs through a running motion: little or no knee lift, kicking out slightly in front of you, and bringing the leg behind.

If you are not feeling much exertion, you're probably lifting the knees too high and moving your legs through a small range of motion. To get the benefit, an extended running motion is needed.

It's important to do water running once a week to keep the adaptations that you have gained. If you miss a week, you should drop back a few minutes from your previous session. If you miss more than 3 weeks, start back at two 5-8 min sessions.

FAT-BURNING AND OVERALL FITNESS EXERCISES

Nordic track

This exercise machine simulates the motion used in cross-country skiing. It is one of the better cross-training modes for fat-burning because it allows you to use a large number of muscle cells while raising body temperature. If you exercise at an easy pace, you can get into the fat-burning zone (past 45 minutes) after a gradual buildup to that amount. This exercise requires no pounding of the legs or feet and (unless you push it too hard or too long) allows you to run as usual the next day.

Rowing machine

There are a number of different types of rowing machines. Some work the legs a bit too hard for runners, but most allow you to use a wide variety of lower and upper body muscle groups. Like the Nordic track, it's possible to exercise for about as long as you wish, once you have gradually worked up to this. Most of the better machines will use a large number of muscle cells, raise body temperature, and can be continued for more than three-quarters of an hour—so they're fat-burners.

Cycling

Indoor cycling (on an exercise cycle) is a better fat-burning exercise than outdoor cycling, because it raises your body temperature a bit more. The muscles used in both indoor and outdoor cycling are mostly the quadraceps muscles—on the front of the upper thigh—reducing the total number of muscle cells compared with the two other modes.

Don't forget walking!

Walking can be done all day long, burning a significant number of calories each day. I call walking a "stealth fat-burner" exercise because it is so easy to walk mile after mile—

especially in small doses. But it is also an excellent cross-training exercise—this includes walking on the treadmill.

CROSS-TRAINING FOR THE UPPER BODY

Weight training

While weight training does not directly benefit running, it can be done on non-running days, or on running days (after a run). There are a wide range of different ways to build strength. If interested, find a coach that can help you build strength in the muscle groups you wish. As mentioned previously in this book, weight training for the legs is not recommended.

Swimming

While not a fat-burner, swimming strengthens the upper body, while improving cardiovascular fitness and endurance in those muscles. Swimming can be done on both running days and non-running days.

Don't Do These on Non-Running Days!

The following exercises will tire the muscles used for running and keep them from recovering between run days. If you really like to do any of these exercises, you can do them after a run, on a running day.

- Stair machines
- Step aerobics
- Weight training for the leg muscles
- Power walking—especially on a hilly course
- Spinning classes (on a bicycle) during which you get out of your seat

Chapter 21

DEALING WITH THE WEATHER

Sometimes, on the snowy, rainy, brutally cold days, I yearn for the early days of running when we had an excuse for not braving the elements. Today, however, there are garments for all weather. Yes, technology has taken away most of our excuses for not exercising. But runners can be very creative. Every year I hear a few new excuses from those who rise to the occasion and find some reason why they can't exercise. In reality, even if you don't have the clothing for hot or cold weather, you can run/walk indoors—on treadmills, in malls or stadiums, or at a gym.

A few years ago, I ran a race in Fairbanks, Alaska. I had to ask the members of the local running club what was the lowest temperature that anyone had endured. The winner had run a 10K in minus 66° F (not wind-chill, this was the real thing: bulb temperature). He said that it really didn't feel that cold. Clothing designers have responded to the needs of runners during extreme weather conditions, making it possible to run, fairly comfortably, in sub-zero conditions. I will admit, however, that if it is minus 66° F, I can't run because I have to rearrange my running shoes next to a warm fire.

HOT WEATHER

I've heard rumors of an air conditioned suit for the heat, but haven't seen it offered by the clothing manufacturers. I could have used this when I ran a marathon in Key West, Florida, when it was 95 degrees for the last 20 miles of the race. After decades of running in hot weather areas, mostly in Florida and Georgia, with some time spent in Hawaii and the Philippines, I haven't found any garments that lower body temperature. The best you can hope for is to minimize the rise, while you feel cooler and a bit more comfortable.

When you exercise strenuously in high heat (above 70°F/19°C), or moderate heat (above 60°F/14°C) with high humidity (above 50%) you raise core body temperature. Most beginning runners will see the internal temperature rise above 55°F (12°C). This triggers a release of blood into the capilliaries of your skin to help cool you down. But this diversion reduces the blood supply available to your exercising muscles, meaning that you will have less blood and less oxygen delivered to the power source that moves you forward—and less blood to move out the waste products from these work sites.

So the bad news is that in warm weather you are going to feel worse and run slower. If you build up the heat too quickly, stay out too long, or run too fast—for you—the result could be heat disease. Make sure that you read the section on this health problem at the end of this chapter. The good news is that you can adapt to these conditions to some extent, as you learn the best time of the day, clothing to wear, and other tricks to keep you cool. But there are some other good options presented, so read on.

Running through the summer heat

1. Run before the sun gets above the horizon. Get up early during warm weather and you will significantly reduce the stress increase due to sunlight. This is particularly a problem in humid areas. Early morning is usually the coolest time of the day, also. Without having to deal with the sun, most runners can gradually adapt to heat. At the very least, your runs will be more enjoyable.

Note: Be sure to take care of safety issues.

2. If you must run when the sun is up, pick a shady course. Shade provides a significant relief in areas of low humidity, and some relief in humid environments.

3. Evening and night runs are usually cooler in areas with low humidity. In humid environments there may not be much relief.

4. Have an indoor facility available. With treadmills, you can exercise in air conditioning. If a treadmill bores you, alternate segments of 5-10 minutes—one segment outdoor, and the next indoor.

5. Don't wear a hat! You lose most of your body heat through the top of your head. Covering the head will cause a quicker internal buildup of heat.

6. Wear light clothing, but not cotton. Many of the new, technical fibers (polypro, coolmax, drifit, etc.) will move moisture away from your skin, producing a cooling effect. Cotton soaks up the sweat, making the garment heavier without providing much of a cooling effect.

7. Pour water over your head. Evaporation not only helps the cooling process—it makes you feel cooler. If you can bring along ice water with you, you will feel a lot cooler as you squirt some regularly over the top of your head.

8. Do your run/walk in installments. It is fine, on a hot day, to put in your 30 minutes by doing 10 in the morning, 10 at noon, and 10 at night. The long run/walk, however, should be done at one time.

9. Take a pool break, or a shower chill-down. During a run, it really helps to take a 2-4 minute dip in a pool or a shower. Some runners in hot areas run loops around their neighborhood and let the hose run over the head each lap. The pool is especially helpful in soaking out excess body temperature. I have run in 97 degree temperatures at our Florida retreat area, breaking up a 5-mile run into 3 x 1.7 mi. Between each, I take a 2-3 minute "soak break" and get back out there. It was only at the end of each segment that I got warm again.

10. Sunscreen—Be sure to protect yourself. Some products, however, produce a coating on the skin, slowing down the perspiration and causing an increase in body temperature buildup. Consult with a dermatologist for your specific needs—or find a product that doesn't block the pores.

11. Drink 6-8 oz of a sports drink like Accelerade or water, at least every 2 hours, or when thirsty, throughout the day during hot weather—when you are not running.

12. Look at the clothing thermometer at the end of this section. Wear loose fitting garments that have some texture in the fabric. Texture will limit or prevent the perspiration from causing a clinging and sticking to the skin.

13. If your only option is going outside on a very hot day, you have my permission to rearrange your running shoes—preferably in front of the air conditioning vent.

Hot weather slowdown for long runs

As the temperature rises above 55°F, your body starts to build up heat, but most runners aren't significantly slowed until 60°F. If you make the adjustments early, you won't have to suffer later and slow down a lot more at that time. The baseline for this table is 60°F or 14°C.

Between 60°F and 65°F	Slow down 30 seconds per mile slower than you would run at 60°F
Between 14°C and 17°C	Slow down 20 seconds per kilometer slower than you would run at 14°C
Between 66°F and 69°F	Slow down 1 minute per mile slower than you would run at 60°F
Between 18°C and 19°C	Slow down 40 seconds per kilometer slower than you would run at 14°C
Between 70°F and 75°F	Slow down 1:30/mile slower than you would run at 60°F
Between 19°C and 22°C	Slow down 1 minute/kilometer slower than you would run at 14°C
Between 76°F and 80°F	Slow down 2 min/mi slower than you would run at 60°F
Between 23°C and 25°C	Slow down 1:20/km slower than you would run at 14°C
Above 80°F and 25°C	Be careful, take extra precautions to avoid heat disease Or....exercise indoors Or....arrange your shoes next to the air conditioner

Note: If you must run speed session on hot days, you can cut the distance of the repetition to 200 meters and do twice as many repetitions. Try to maintain pace. Cool off between reps by pouring cold water over your head as you walk for half a lap between each. Monitor signs of heat disease and don't keep pushing into this condition.

Heat Disease Alert!

While it is unlikely that you will push yourself into heat disease, the longer you are exercising in hot (and/or humid) conditions, the more you increase the likelihood of this dangerous medical situation. That's why I recommend breaking up your exercise into short segments when it's hot and you must run outdoors. Be sensitive to your reactions to the heat, and those of the runners around you. When one of the symptoms is present, this is normally not a major problem unless there is significant distress. But when several are experienced, take action because heat disease can lead to death. It's always better to be conservative: stop the workout, cool off, and get help if needed.

Heat Disease Symptoms

- Intense heat buildup in the head

- General overheating of the body

- Significant headache

- Significant nausea or vomiting

- General confusion and loss of concentration

- Loss of muscle control

- Excessive sweating and then cessation of sweating

- Clammy skin

- Excessively rapid breathing

- Muscle cramps

- Feeling faint

- Diarrhea

Heat Disease Risk Factors

- Viral or bacterial infection

- Taking medication—especially cold medicines, diuretics, medicines for diarrhea, antihistamines, atropine, scopolamine, tranquilizers

- Dehydration (especially due to alcohol)

- Severe sunburn

- Overweight

- Lack of heat training

- Exercising more than one is used to

- Occurrence of heat disease in the past

- Several nights of extreme sleep deprivation

- Certain medical conditions including high cholesterol, high blood pressure, extreme stress, asthma, diabetes, epilepsy, drug use (including alcohol), cardiovascular disease, smoking, or a general lack of fitness

Take action! Call 911

Use your best judgment, but in most cases anyone who exhibits two or more of the symptoms should get into a cool environment, and receive medical attention immediately. An extremely effective cool off method is to soak towels, sheets or clothing in cool, icy water, and wrap them around the individual. If ice is available, sprinkle some ice over the wet cloth.

Heat adaptation workout

If you gradually increase the amount you exercise in hot weather, your body will get better at dealing with it. As with all training components, it is important to do this regularly. You should be sweating to some extent at the end of the workout, although the amount and the duration of perspiration is an individual issue. If the heat (and/or humidity) is particularly high, cut back the amount.

Important Note: Read the section on heat disease and stop this workout if you sense that you are even beginning to become nauseous, lose concentration or mental awareness of your condition, etc.

- Done on a short running day once a week

- Do the run-walk ratio that you usually use, going at a comfortable pace (walkers walk slowly)

- Warm up with a 5-min gentle walk and take a 5-min gentle walk cool-down

- Temperature should be between 75°F and 85°F (22-27°C) for best results

- Stop at the first sign of nausea or significant heat stress

- When less than 70°F (19°C), you can put on additional layers of clothing to simulate a higher temperature

- First session, run-walk for only 3-4 minutes in the heat

- Each successive session, add 2-3 minutes

Tip: Maintaining heat tolerance during the winter

By putting on additional layers of clothing so that you sweat within 3-4 minutes of your run-walk, you can keep much of your summer heat conditioning. Continue to run for a total of 5-12 minutes at an easy pace.

DEALING WITH THE COLD

While most of my runs have been in temperatures above 60°F, I've also run in minus 30. I prepared for this run extensively and put on about as many layers as I had in my suitcase. When I met my winter running guide for the run he quickly evaluated my clothing and found me lacking. After another two layers I was ready to go.

The specific type of garments, especially the one next to your skin, is an individual issue. I'm not going to get into the specifics here because the technology changes quickly. In general, you want your first layer to be comfortable and not too thick. There are a number of fabrics today, mostly synthetic, that hold a comfortable amount of body heat, close to the skin to keep you warm, but don't let you overheat. Most of these same fibers allow for moisture such as perspiration and rain, to be moved away from the skin—even as you run and walk. Not only does this add to your comfort in winter, but almost eliminates a chill due to having wet skin underneath.

Running through the chill of winter

1. Expand your lunch hour if you want to run outdoors. Midday is usually the warmest time of the day, so you will probably have to plan to arrive at work early (pay bills, run errands, etc.). The midday sun can make your outdoor running much more comfortable—even when it is very cold.

2. If early morning is the only time you can run, bundle up. The "clothing thermometer" at the end of this section will help you to dress for the temperature and not overdress.

3. Run into the wind at the start, particularly when you are running out and turning around. If you run with the wind at your back for the first half of the run you'll tend to sweat. When you turn into a cold wind, you'll chill down dramatically.

4. Having a health club will give you an indoor venue and other exercise options. With treadmills, you can run without wind chill. I have worked with many runners who hate running on treadmills, but also hate running for more than 15 minutes in the cold. Their solution is to alternate segments of 7-15 minutes—one segment outdoor, and the next indoor. Count the transition as a walk break. Health clubs expand your exercise horizons offering a variety of alternative exercise.

5. One of your exercise days could be a triathlon—your choice of three exercises. You can do exercises out of your home, or at a health club.

6. Seek out a large indoor facility near your office or home. In Houston, runners use the tunnels below city streets. Many northern cities offer skyways and allow runners and walkers to use them when traffic allows it. Domes, malls, and civic centers often allow winter runners and walkers at certain times.

7. Wear a hat! You lose most of your body heat through the top of your head. Covering the head will help you retain body heat and stay warm.

8. Cover your extremities from the wind chill you produce when you run and walk in the cold! Protect ears, and hands, nose and generally the front of the face. Make sure that you protect the feet with socks that are thick enough. And men, wear an extra pair of underwear.

9. Do your run-walk in installments. It is fine, on a really cold day, to put in your 30 minutes by doing 10 in the morning, 10 at noon and 10 at night.

10. Take a "warm-up" break. Before you head out into the cold, walk and run in place, indoors. On a really cold day take your walk breaks indoors.

11. Vasoline—be sure to protect yourself wherever there is exposed skin on very cold days. One area, for example, is the skin around the eyes, not protected by a ski mask, etc.

12. When you are exercising during the winter, indoor or outdoor, you will be losing almost as much in sweat as in the warm months. You should still drink at least 4-6 oz of a sports drink like Accelerade or water, at least every 2 hours, or when thirsty, throughout the day (when not running). During a long run, the recommended fluid intake is between 14 and 27 oz an hour.

13. Another reminder: Look at the clothing thermometer at the end of this section and customize it for your situation.

CLOTHING THERMOMETER

After years of working with people in various climates, here are my recommendations for the appropriate clothing based upon the temperature. As always, however, wear what works best for you. The general rule is to choose your garments by function first. And remember that the most important layer for comfort is the one next to your skin. Garments made out of fabric labeled Polypro, coolmax, drifit, etc., hold enough body heat close to you in winter, while releasing extra heat. In summer and winter, they move moisture away from the skin—cooling you in hot weather, and avoiding a chill in the winter.

Temperature	What to wear
14°C or 60°F and above	Tank top and shorts (or compression shorts to avoid chaffing)
9 to 13°C or 50 to 59°F	T-shirt and shorts (or compression shorts to avoid chaffing)
5 to 8°C or 40 to 49°F	Lightweight, long-sleeve shirt, shorts or tights (or nylon long pants), mittens and gloves
0 to 4°C or 30 to 39°F	Medium-weight, long-sleeve shirt, and another T-shirt, tights and shorts, socks or mittens or gloves and a hat over the ears
−4 to −1°C or 20 to 29°F	Medium-weight, long-sleeve shirt, another T-shirt, tights and shorts, socks, mittens or gloves, and a hat over the ears

−8 to −3°C or 10 to 19°F	Medium-weight, long-sleeve shirt, and medium/heavyweight shirt, tights and shorts, nylon windsuit, top and pants, socks, thick mittens, and a hat over the ears
−12° to −7°C or 0° to 9°F	Two medium- or heavyweight, long-sleeve tops, thick tights, thick underwear (especially for men), medium to heavy warm-up suit, gloves and thick mittens, ski mask, a hat over the ears, and Vaseline covering any exposed skin
−18° to −11°C or −15°F	Two heavyweight, long-sleeve tops, tights and thick tights, thick underwear (and supporter for men), thick warm-up (top and pants), mittens over gloves, thick ski mask and a hat over ears, Vasoline covering any exposed skin, thicker socks on your feet and other foot protection, as needed
−20° both C & F	Add layers as needed

What Not to Wear

1. A heavy coat in winter. If the layer is too thick, you'll heat up, sweat excessively, and cool too much when you take it off.

2. No shirt for men in summer. Fabric that holds some of the moisture will give you more of a cooling effect as you run and walk.

3. Too much sunscreen—it can interfere with sweating.

4. Socks that are too thick in summer. Your feet swell and the pressure from the socks can increase the chance of a black toenail and blisters.

5. Lime green shirt with bright pink dots (unless you have a lot of confidence and/or can run fast).

TROUBLESHOOTING

HOW DO I START BACK AFTER HAVING HAD TIME OFF?

The longer you've been away from exercise, the slower you must return. I want to warn you now that you will reach a point when you feel totally back in shape—but you are not. Stay with the following plan for your return and when in doubt, be more conservative. Remember that you are in this for the long run!

Less than 2 weeks off: You will feel like you are starting over again, but should come back quickly. Let's say that you were at week 10, but had to take 10 days off. Start back at week 2 for the first week. If all is well, skip to week 3 or 4 for the second week. If that works well, gradually transition back to the schedule you were using before you had your layoff, over the next 2 weeks.

14 days to 29 days off: You will also feel like you are starting over again, and it will take longer to get it all back. Within about 5-6 weeks you should be back to normal. Use the schedule of your choice (from week 1) for two weeks. If there are no aches, pains, or lingering fatigue, then use the schedule but skip every other week. After the 5th week, transition back into what you were doing before the layoff.

One month or more off: If you have not run for a month or more, start over again, like a beginner. Use the "To Finish" schedules in this book, following them exactly (from week 1) for the first few weeks. After 2-3 weeks, the safest plan is to continue with the schedule. But if you're having no aches and pains, and no lingering fatigue, you could increase more rapidly by skipping one week out of three. After 2 months of no problems, your conditioning will have returned.

IT HURTS! IS IT JUST A PASSING ACHE, OR A REAL INJURY?

Most of the aches and pains you feel during exercise will go away within minute or two. If the pain comes on during a workout, just walk very gently for an additional 2 minutes, then ease back into your pace. If the pain comes back after doing this 4 or 5 times, stop the workout.

Walking pain

When the pain stays around when walking, try a very short stride. Walk for a 30-60 seconds. If it still hurts when walking, try sitting down, and massaging the area that hurts, if you can. Sit for 2-4 minutes. When you try again to walk, and it still hurts, call it a day—your workout is over.

IT'S AN INJURY IF....

There's inflammation—swelling in the area
There's loss of function—the foot, knee, etc. doesn't work correctly
There's pain—it hurts and keeps hurting or gets worse

Treatment suggestions

1. See a doctor who has treated other exercisers very successfully and wants to get you back on the road or trail.

2. Take at least 2-5 days off from any activity that could irritate the area, to get the healing started. Take more time if needed.

3. If the area is next to the skin (tendon, foot, etc.), rub a chunk of ice on the area(s)—constantly rubbing for 15 min until the area gets numb. Continue to do this for a week after you feel no symptoms. Ice bags and gel ice do no good at all in most cases.

4. If the problem is inside a joint or muscle, call your doctor and ask if you can use prescription strength anti-inflammatory medication. Don't take any medication without a doctor's advice—and follow that advice.

5. If you have a muscle injury, see a veteran sports massage therapist. Try to find one who has a lot of successful experience treating the area where you are injured. The magic fingers and hands can often work wonders.

This is advice from one exerciser to another. For more info on injuries, treatment, etc. see a doctor and read the "injury free" chapter in this book, and *Galloway's Book on Running*.

NO ENERGY TODAY

There will be several days each year when you will not feel like exercising. On most of these, you can turn your mood around and feel great. Occasionally, you will not be able to do this, because of an infection, lingering fatigue, or other physical problems. Here's a list of things that can give you energy. If these actions don't get you out the door, then read the nutrition sections—particularly the blood sugar chapter in this book—and in *Galloway's Book on Running*.

1. Eat an energy bar, with water or caffeinated beverage, about an hour before the workout. Caffeine helps!

2. Instead of #1, half an hour before exercising, you could drink 100-200 calories of a sports drink that has a mix of 80% simple carbohydrate and 20% protein. The product Accelerade has this already put together.

3. Just walk for 5 minutes away from your house, office, etc., and the energy often kicks in. Forward movement helps the attitude.

4. One of the prime reasons for no energy is that you didn't reload within 30 minutes after your last exercise session: 200-300 calories of a mix that is 80% simple carbohydrate and 20% protein (Endurox R4 is the product that has this formulated).

5. Low-carb diets will result in low energy before a workout, and often no energy to finish the workout.

6. In most cases it is fine to keep going even if you aren't energetic. But if you sense an infection, see a doctor. If the low energy stays around for several days, see a nutritionist that knows about the special needs of exercisers and/or get some blood work done. This may be due to inadequate iron, B vitamins, energy stores, etc.

Note: If you have any problems with caffeine, don't consume any products containing it. As always, if you sense any health problem, see a doctor.

SIDE PAIN

This is very common among runners, and usually has a simple fix. Normally it is not anything to worry about...it just hurts. Normally, I've found that this condition is due to 1) the lack of deep breathing, and 2) going a little too fast at the beginning of the run. You can correct #2 easily by walking more at the beginning, and slowing down your running pace.

Lower lung breathing from the beginning of a run can prevent side pain. This way of inhaling air is performed by diverting the air you breathe into your lower lungs. Also called "belly breathing" this is how we breathe when asleep, and it provides maximum opportunity for oxygen absorption. If you don't deep breathe when you run, then you are probably not getting as much oxygen as you could. The side pain will tell you. By slowing down, walking, and breathing deeply for a while, the pain may go away. But sometimes it does not. Most runners just continue to run and walk with the side pain. In 50 years of running and helping others run, I've not seen any lasting negative effect from those who run with this type of side pain.

You don't have to take in a maximum breath to perform this technique. Simply breathe a normal breath but send it to the lower lungs. You know that you have done this if your stomach goes up and down as you inhale and exhale. If your chest goes up and down, and your stomach does not, you are using primarily the upper lungs.

Note: Never breathe in and out rapidly. This can lead to hyperventilation, dizziness, and fainting.

I FEEL GREAT ONE DAY BUT NOT THE NEXT

If you can completely solve this problem, you could become a very wealthy person. There are a few common reasons for this, but there will always be "those days" when the body doesn't seem to work right—the gravity seems heavier than normal—and you cannot find a reason.

1. Pushing through. In most cases, this is a one-day occurrence. Most runners just put more walking into the mix, and get through it. Walkers take more shuffle breaks. Before you try to push through tiredness, however, make sure that there's not a medical reason for your state of mind. Don't exercise when you have a lung infection, for example.

2. Heat or humidity will make you feel worse. You will often feel great when the temperature is below 60°F and miserable when 80°F or above (especially at the end of the workout).

3. Low blood sugar can make any run a bad run/walk. You may feel good at the start and suddenly feel like you have no energy. Every step seems to take a major effort. Read the chapter in this book about this topic.

4. Low motivation. Use the rehearsal techniques in the "staying motivated" chapter to get you out the door on a bad day. These have helped numerous exercisers turn their minds around—even in the middle of a workout.

5. Infection can leave you feeling lethargic, achy, and unable to exercise at a pace that was easy a few days earlier. Check the normal signs (fever, chills, swollen lymph glands, etc.) and at least call your doctor if you suspect something.

6. Medication and alcohol, even when taken the day before, can leave a hangover that dampens a workout.

7. A slower start can make the difference between a good day and a bad day. When your body is on the edge of fatigue or other stress, it only takes a few seconds too fast per mile, walking and/or running, to push into discomfort or worse.

CRAMPS IN THE MUSCLES

At some point, most people who run experience cramps (and some walkers do, also). These muscle contractions usually occur in the feet or the calf muscles and may come during a run or walk, or they may hit at random. Most commonly, they will occur at night, or when you are sitting around at your desk or watching TV in the afternoon or evening.

Cramps vary in severity. Most are mild but some can grab so hard that they shut down the muscles and hurt when they seize up. Massage and a short and gentle movement of the muscle can help to bring most of the cramps around. Odds are that stretching will make the cramp worse, or tear the muscle fibers.

Most cramps are due to overuse—exercising farther or faster than in the recent past, or continuing to put yourself at your limit, especially in warm weather. Look at the pace and distance of your runs and walks in your training journal to see if you have been going too far, or too fast, or both.

- Continuous running increases cramping. Taking walk breaks more often can reduce or eliminate cramps. Many runners who used to cramp when they ran a minute and walked a minute, stopped cramping with a ratio of run 30 seconds and walk 30-60 seconds. Walkers can reduce cramping by using shuffle breaks.

- During hot weather, a good electrolyte beverage can help to replace the salts that you lose in sweating (the day before and the day after a long or hard run or walk). A drink like Accelerade, for example, can help to top off these minerals when you drink about 6-8 oz every 1-2 hours.

- On very long hikes, walks, or runs, however, the continuous sweating, especially when drinking a lot of fluid, can push your sodium levels too low and produce muscle cramping. If this happens regularly, a buffered salt tablet has helped greatly: Succeed.

- Many medications, especially those designed to lower cholesterol, have as one of their known side effects, muscle cramps. Runners who use medications and cramp should ask their doctor if there are alternatives.

Here are several ways of dealing with cramps

1. Take a longer and more gentle warm-up

2. Shorten your run segment

3. Slow down your walk, and walk more

4. Shorten your distance on a hot/humid day

5. Break your run up into two segments

6. Look at any other exercise that could be causing the cramps

7. Take a buffered salt tablet at the beginning of your exercise

8. Shorten your stride—especially on hills

> **Note:** If you have high blood pressure, ask your doctor before taking any salt product.

UPSET STOMACH OR DIARRHEA

Sooner or later, virtually every runner, or long distance walker, has at least one episode with nausea or diarrhea. It comes from the buildup of total stress. Most commonly, it is the stress of running/walking on that day, due to the following causes. But stress can come from many unique conditions within the individual. Your body triggers the nausea/diarrhea to get you to reduce the exercise, which will reduce the stress. Here are the common causes.

1. **Running too fast or too far** (walking too far) are the most common causes. Runners are confused about this, because the pace doesn't feel too fast in the beginning. Each person has a level of fatigue that triggers these conditions. Slowing down and taking more walk breaks will help you manage the problem.

2. **Eating too much or too soon before the workout.** Your system has to work hard when you're running/walking, and must also work hard to digest food. Doing both at the same time raises stress and results in nausea, etc. Having food in your stomach in the process of being digested is an extra stress and a likely target for elimination.

3. **Eating a high fat or high protein diet.** Even one meal that has over 50% of the calories in fat or protein can lead to N/D hours later.

4. **Eating too much the afternoon or evening, the day before.** A big evening meal will still be in the gut the next morning, being digested. When you bounce up and down on a run, which you will, you add stress to the system often producing nausea/diarrhea (N/D).

5. **Heat and humidity** are a major cause of these problems. Some people don't adapt to heat well and experience N/D with minimal buildup of temperature or humidity. But in hot conditions, everyone has a core body temperature increase that will result in significant stress to the system—often causing nausea, and sometimes diarrhea. By slowing down, taking more walk (or shuffle) breaks, and pouring water over your head, you can manage this better. The best time to exercise in warm weather is before the sun gets above the horizon.

6. **Drinking too much water before a run or walk.** If you have too much water in your stomach, and you are bouncing around, you put stress on the digestive system.

Reduce your intake to the bare minimum. Most exercisers don't need to drink any fluid before a workout that is 60 minutes or less.

7. **Drinking too much of a sugar/electrolyte drink.** Water is the easiest substance for the body to process. The addition of sugar and/or electrolyte minerals, as in a sports drink, makes the substance harder to digest for many exercisers. During a run/walk (especially on a hot day) it is best to drink only water. Cold water is best.

8. **Drinking too much fluid too soon after a run or walk.** Even if you are very thirsty, don't gulp down large quantities of any fluid. Try to drink no more than 6-8 oz, every 20 minutes or so. If you are particularly prone to this N/D, just take 2-4 sips, every 5 minutes or so. When the body is very stressed and tired, it's not a good idea to consume a sugar drink. The extra stress of digesting the sugar can lead to problems.

9. **Don't let workouts be stressful to you.** Some runners or walkers get too obsessed about getting their workout at a specific pace. This adds stress to your life. Relax and let your exercise diffuse some of the other tensions in your life.

HEADACHE

There are several reasons why long distance exercisers get headaches after workouts. While uncommon, they happen to the average runner about 1-5 times a year. The extra stress that running puts on the body can trigger a headache on a tough day—even considering the relaxation that comes from the run. Walkers can experience the headaches after long walks that take more than 2 hours—especially in the heat. Many runners find that a dose of an over-the-counter headache medication takes care of the problem. As always, consult with your doctor about use of medication. Here are the causes/solutions.

Dehydration—If you exercise in the morning, make sure that you hydrate well the day before. Avoid alcohol if you work out in the mornings and have headaches. Also watch the salt in your dinner meal the night before. A good sports drink like accelerade, taken throughout the day the day before, will help to keep your fluid levels and your electrolytes "topped off". If you run/walk in the afternoon, follow the same advice leading up to your workout.

Medications can often produce dehydration—There are some medications that make exercisers more prone to headaches. Check with your doctor.

Too hot for you—Run at a cooler time of the day (usually in the morning before the sun gets above the horizon). When on a hot run or walk, pour water over your head.

Running a little too fast—Start all runs more slowly, walk more during the first half of the run.

Going farther than you have run in the recent past—Monitor your mileage and don't increase more than about 15% farther than you have run on any single run/walk in the past week.

Low blood sugar level—Be sure that you boost your BLS with a snack, about 30-60 min before you exercise. If you are used to having it, caffeine in a beverage can sometimes help this situation also.

If prone to migranes—Generally avoid caffeine, and try your best to avoid dehydration. Talk to your doctor about other possibilities.

Watch your neck and lower back—If you have a slight forward lean as you run or walk, you can put pressure on the spine—particularly in the neck and lower back. Read the form chapter in this book and try to maintain upright posture.

SHOULD I RUN WHEN I HAVE A COLD?

There are so many individual health issues with a cold that you should talk with a doctor before you exercise when you have an infection. Usually you will be given the OK to gently exercise.

Lung infection—don't exercise! A virus in the lungs can move into the heart, which may produce degenerative damage or death. Lung infections are usually indicated by coughing. Don't take a chance—rest and get well.

Common cold? There are many infections that initially seem to be a normal cold but are not. At least call your doctor's office to get clearance before exercising. Be sure to explain your current training level, what you would like to do, and what, if any medication you are taking.

Throat infection and above—Most runners/walkers will be given the OK, but check with the doc.

STREET SAFETY

Each year several runners/walkers are hit by cars when running. Most of these are preventable. Here are the primary reasons and what you can do about them.

1. **The driver is intoxicated or preoccupied by cellphone, etc.**

    Always be on guard—even when running/walking on the sidewalk or pedestrian trail. Most of the fatal crashes I've heard about, occurred when the driver lost control of the car, hitting the victim from behind. I know it is wonderful to be on "cruise control" in your right brain, but you can avoid a life threatening situation if you stay vigilant, and anticipate.

2. **The runner/walker dashes across an intersection against the traffic light**

    When running or walking with another person, don't try to follow blindly across an intersection. Runners who quickly sprint across the street without looking are often surprised by cars coming from unexpected directions. The best rule is the one that you heard as a child: When you get to an intersection, stop, see what the traffic situation is. Look both ways, and look both ways again (and again) before crossing. Have an option to bail out of the crossing if a car surprises you from any direction.

3. **Sometimes, runners/walkers wander out into the street as they exercise together**

    One of the very positive aspects of running/walking becomes a negative one, in this case. Yes, chat and enjoy time with your friends. But every person in a group needs to be responsible for his or her own safety, footing, etc. The biggest mistake I see is that those at the back of a group assume that they don't have to be concerned about traffic at all. This lack of concern is a very risky situation.

In general, be ready to save yourself from a variety of traffic problems by following the rules below and any others that apply to specific situations.

- Be constantly aware of vehicular traffic, at all times.

- Assume that all drivers are drunk or crazy or both. When you see a strange movement by a car, be ready to get out of the way.

- Mentally practice running for safety. Get into the practice of thinking ahead at all times, with a plan for that current stretch of road.

- Run/walk as far off the road as you can. If possible exercise on a sidewalk or pedestrian trail.

- Run facing traffic. A high percentage of traffic deaths come from those who are moving with the flow of traffic, and do not see the threat from behind.

- Wear white clothes and reflective gear at night. I've heard the accounts and this apparel has saved lives.

- Take control over your safety—you are the only one on the road who will usually save yourself.

PERSONAL SAFETY

Take charge by thinking ahead and being aware of your surroundings.

- Bring a shrill whistle with you

- In uncertain areas, bring pepper spray

- Bring a cell phone, and call someone if you feel threatened

- Wear an ID tag on your shoe

- Tell someone where you will be running, and when you should be back

- Use your instincts—turn around if you feel uneasy on a certain street

- It's best not to wear any device in your ear, but if you do, keep the sound as low as possible and one ear uncovered

- If threatened, swing your elbow at the head of the attacker, put fingers in the eyes, kick in the groin

DOGS

When you enter a dog's territory, you may be in for a confrontation. Here are my suggestions for dealing with your "dog days":

1. There are several good devices that will help deter dogs: an old fashioned stick, rocks, and some electronic signal devices, and pepper spray. If you are in a new area, or an area of known dogs, I recommend that you have one of these at all times.

2. At the first sign of a dog ahead, or barking, try to figure out where the dog is located, whether the dog is a real threat, and what territory the dog is guarding.

3. The best option is to use a different route.

4. If you really want or need to go past the dog, pick up a rock if you don't have another anti-dog device.

5. Watch the tail. If the tail does not wag, beware.

6. As you approach the dog it is natural for the dog to bark and head toward you. Raise your rock as if you will throw it at the dog. In my experience, the dog withdraws about 90% of the time. You may need to do this several times before getting through the dog's territory. Keep your arms up.

7. In a few cases you will need to throw the rock, and sometimes another if the dog keeps coming.

8. In less that 1% of the hundreds of dog confrontations I've had, there is something wrong with the dog, and it continues to move toward you. Usually the hair will be up on the dog's back. Try to find a barrier to get behind, yell loudly in hopes that the owner or someone will help you. If a car comes by, try to flag down the driver, and either stay behind the car as you get out of the dog's territory, or get in the car for protection if that is appropriate.

9. Develop your own voice. Some use a deep commanding voice, some use a high pitched voice. Whichever you use, exude confidence and command.

Chapter 23

TROUBLESHOOTING ACHES AND PAINS

It is always better to take 2-3 days off from running/walking, and then start back gently if you sense that you may be acquiring an injury. In most of these "weak link" pain sites, I've found that stretching aggravates the problem. For more information, see GALLOWAY'S BOOK ON RUNNING.

SHINS: SORENESS OR PAIN IN THE FRONT OF THE SHIN (ANTERIOR TIBIAL AREA)

Note: Even after you make the corrections, shin problems often take several weeks to heal. As long as the shin problem is not a stress fracture, easy exercise can often allow it to heal as quickly (or more quickly) than complete layoff. In general, most runners/walkers can exercise when they have shin splints—they just need to stay below the threshold of further irritation.

Causes:

1. Increasing too rapidly—just walk more gently for 1-2 weeks, and walk with a short stride, gently.

2. Running/walking too fast, even on one day—when in doubt, run slower/walk slower on all runs.

3. Running or walking with a stride that is too long—shorten stride and use more of a "shuffle".

SORENESS OR PAIN AT THE INSIDE OF THE LOWER LEG (POSTERIOR TIBIAL AREA)

Causes

1. Same three causes as in anterior tibial shin splints.

2. More common with runners and walkers who overpronate. This means that they tend to roll to the inside of the foot as they push off.

3. Shoes may be too soft, allowing a floppy/pronated foot to roll inward more than usual.

Corrections:

1. Reduce stride length.

2. Runners: Slow the pace at the beginning and insert more walking from the beginning.

3. If you are an overpronator on the forward part of your feet, try on a stable, motion control shoe.

4. Ask your foot doctor if there is a foot device that can help you.

SHOULDER AND NECK MUSCLES TIRED AND TIGHT

Primary Cause:
Leaning too far forward as you run or walk.

Other Causes:

1. Holding arms too far away from the body as you exercise.

2. Swinging arms and shoulders too much as you exercise.

Corrections:

1. Use the "puppet on a string" image (detailed in the running form chapter) about every 4-5 minutes during all runs and walks—particularly the longer ones. This is noted in the section on posture.

2. Watch how you are holding your arms. Try to keep the arms close to the body, relaxed.

3. Minimize the swing of your arms. Keep the hands close to the body, lightly touching your shirt or the outside of your shorts as your arms swing.

LOWER BACK: TIGHT, SORE, OR PAINFUL AFTER A RUN/WALK

Causes

1. Leaning too far forward.

2. Having a stride length that is too long for you.

Corrections:

1. Use the "puppet on a string image several times on all runs and walks—particularly the longer ones. This is noted in the chapter on running form, in the section on posture.

2. Ask a physical therapist whether some strengthening exercise can help.

3. When in doubt, shorten your stride length.

4. For more information, see GALLOWAY'S BOOK ON RUNNING

KNEE PAIN AT THE END OF A RUN/WALK

Causes:

1. Stride length could be too long.

2. Doing too much, too soon.

3. Not inserting enough walk breaks (or shuffle breaks), regularly, from the beginning.

4. When the main running muscles get tired, you will tend to wobble from side to side.

Corrections:

1. Shorten stride.

2. Stay closer to the ground, using more of a shuffle.

3. Monitor your mileage in a log book, and hold your increase to less than 10% a week.

4. Use more walk breaks during your run (shuffle breaks in a walk).

5. Start at a slower pace.

BEHIND THE KNEE: PAIN, TIGHTNESS, OR CONTINUED SORENESS OR WEAKNESS

Causes:

1. Stretching.

2. Overstriding—particularly at the end of the workout.

Corrections:

1. Don't stretch.

2. Keep your stride length under control.

3. Keep feet low to the ground.

HAMSTRINGS: TIGHTNESS, SORENESS, OR PAIN

Causes:

1. Stretching.

2. Stride length too long.

3. Lifting the foot too high behind, as your leg swings back.

Corrections:

1. Don't stretch.

2. Maintain a short stride, keeping the hamstring relaxed—especially at the end of the workout.

3. Take more walking/shuffling early in the workout, possibly throughout to stay below irritation.

4. As the leg swings behind you, let the lower leg rise no higher than a position that is parallel to the horizontal before swinging forward again (avoid the back-kick).

5. Deep tissue massage can sometimes help with this muscle group.

QUADRACEPS (FRONT OF THE THIGH): SORE, TIRED, PAINFUL

Causes:

1. Lifting your knee too high—especially when tired.

2. Using the quads to slow down going downhill—because you were going too fast, or with a stride that was too long.

Corrections:

1. Maintain little or no knee lift—especially at the end of your workout.

2. Run with a shuffle, walk with a "walk-shuffle" (see the walking form chapter).

3. Let your stride get very short at the top of hills, and when tired—don't lengthen it.

4. If you are going too fast downhill, keep shortening stride until you slow down.

5. Take more walk breaks (shuffle breaks) on the downhill.

SORE FEET OR LOWER LEGS

Causes:

1. Too much bounce.

2. Pushing off too hard.

3. Shoes don't fit correctly or are too worn out.

4. Insole of shoe is worn out.

Corrections:

1. Keep feet low to the ground.

2. Maintain a light touch of the feet.

3. Get a shoe check to see if your shoes are too worn.

4. You may need only a new insole.

Chapter 24

MAJOR DIFFERENCES AS YOU GET OLDER

"With the right adjustments in pace and walk/shuffle breaks, almost any exerciser can reduce injury as the years go by".

Every year I hear dozens of people tell me that they wish they could run, but they didn't start doing it when they were younger—and felt it was too late for them. Within a few minutes, these folks wish they hadn't said that to me. I work with hundreds of people every year who are in their 40s, 50s, 60s, 70s, and even 80s who are taking their first steps. Most of these folks become runners within 6 months. Many of them finish marathons— yes, even the 80 year olds—within a year.

The principles of training which are described in this book apply to everyone—at any age. If you add a little stress followed by rest for recovery, your body rebuilds stronger.

The psychological rewards are the same at any age. Endorphins make your muscles feel better. You have a better attitude all day—after a workout. Each one can bring a special relaxation not bestowed by other activities.

ELLIOTT GALLOWAY

As my father got more obese in his 40s, and more out of shape, he gave me every excuse one can imagine why he couldn't exercise. By his 50th birthday, even I had pretty much given up on trying to get him to exert himself. His "reality check" was a high school reunion.

Out of 25 guys who had been on his football team, only 12 were alive at age 52. As he drove home, the advice of his doctor, myself, and others came back to him. He realized that he could be the next to depart this world, at a time when he was just getting into his life's work—the founding of an innovative school.

The former all-state athlete was shocked on his first workout, when he could only run about 100 yards before his legs gave out on him. But he stuck with it. Every other day his mission was to run to one more telephone pole before walking back. Within a year he was regularly running around the golf course in front of his office, 3 miles. A year after that, he completed the Peachtree Road Race 10K. After another 3 years' training, he ran faster than 40 minutes in the 10K. I'm most proud of the fact that in his mid-80s, my dad walked and ran over 20 miles a week.

Today I work with dozens of runners who consider themselves "over the hill", but accomplish some amazing things. Even the 80+ year old beginners get caught up in the excitement of getting more fit. They cannot believe how much better they feel—every day. Honestly,

these people are my heros. I hope I can be like them when I grow up.

RECOVERY SLOWS DOWN AFTER 40

Having run since I was 13, I've noticed subtle changes that are usually not noticeable year to year. It's only when I now look back over almost 5 decades of running that I see the trends.

1. Your recovery rate slows down each year past the age of 40

2. At the same time, your mental focus has increased so you can push yourself further into fatigue

3. By the age of 55, there has been a significant slowdown from the age of 40

4. By the age of 65, another significant slowdown has occurred—even from 55

5. Continuing to train the same way every year, will produce injuries, lingering fatigue, or burnout

6.   It takes longer to warm up for each run

7.   Any type of fast running, for you, will greatly increase the time needed for recovery, and injury risk

NO OVERUSE INJURIES IN ALMOST 30 YEARS

I began to notice increasing and continuous leg fatigue as I approached my 40th birthday, when I was running 6-7 days a week. So I decided to follow the advice I was giving to other 40+ runners who felt the same way: run every other day. In about 4 weeks, my legs were fresh again. But after 2 years of getting in only 3 runs a week, I needed more endorphins—I wanted to run more. Gradually I added more days. Now, I'm past 60, but running almost every day.

How is it then, that I enjoy running more now than ever, even when running each day? It's because I am running much slower and taking walk breaks very frequently. At the start of every run, I take a walk break about every minute. After about 3 miles I'm usually walking about every 3-4 minutes, but sometimes still at one minute. I adjust to how my body feels that day. I haven't had to take more than two days off from running in almost 3 decades.

HOW TO DEAL WITH THE RECOVERY RATE SLOWDOWN FOR RUNNERS

After the age of 35, it takes longer for the legs to feel fresh and bouncy after a strenuous run. Most runners don't notice this (or don't want to admit it) until they reach the age of 40. By adding conservative training ingredients, injury risk drops dramatically. Many veterans find that they run faster while covering fewer miles per week—especially when running fewer days per week.

The best way we've found to speed recovery is to include strategic rest days before and after strenuous exercise days. This allows the body to rebuild and adapt to efficient running. In general, it is better to cover more miles on certain key days and then avoid the use of the same muscles, the next day (cross-training is fine). The following table has recommendations for the number of days one can run, based upon age, for runners who:

●   Are experiencing more injuries, aches and pains, or orthopedic problems

●   Are not recovering quickly between the more difficult sessions

●   Are experiencing a slowdown in race times [If you're not having any of these problems you can run the number of days per week that you wish]

Recommended number of running days per week by age:
(You can walk or cross train on most other days if desired)

35 and under: no more than 5 days a week
36-45: no more than 4 days a week
46-59: every other day
60+: 3 days a week
70+: 2 longer run days and 1 walk day (or a water running day
80+: One longer run/walk, one shorter run/walk, and one very easy short walk (or water running day)

Note: **The day before the long run should be a day of rest.**

MORE WALK BREAKS

The simple addition of more walk breaks, from the beginning of exercise, has allowed many mature runners to maintain mileage while reducing aches and pains.

ADJUSTMENTS FOR RUNNERS

Run pace (minutes/mile)	Minutes running/Minutes walking
8:00	Run 4 min/Walk 30 sec
8:30	Run 3 min/Walk 30 sec
9:00	Run 2 min/Walk 30 sec
10:00	Run 1:30 min/Walk 30 sec
11:00-12:00	Run 1 min/Walk 30 sec
13:00-14:00	Run 30 sec/Walk 30 sec OR 20/20 OR 15/15
15:00	Run 15 sec/Walk 30 sec
16:00	Run 10 sec/Walk 30 sec

A LONGER AND EASIER WARM-UP

As the years go by, it takes longer (during an individual run or walk) for the legs to feel good. Here is what I recommend:

- At least 5 minutes of very gentle walking

- Then, 5 minutes of walking at varied paces. Even if you walk a bit faster during the second 5 minutes, use a short stride.

- Runners will then insert some run breaks into your walk for 10 minutes. Start with 10-20 seconds of running followed by a minute of walking, then gradually shift to a minute of running and a minute of walking—or 30 sec/30 sec. Walkers will then settle into their walk/shuffle pace for the day.

- Runners should then, ease into your running pace, and the run-walk-run frequency for that day.

- It is always better to be conservative—walk or shuffle more frequently if needed.

BREAKING UP YOUR DAILY MILEAGE INTO 2 OR 3 SESSIONS

A runner recently told me that her fitness improved during the year after she retired from her career in nursing. Instead of walking her 3 miles once a day, she walked 2 miles in the morning and 2-3 miles in the afternoon. She enjoyed the vitality boost from both sessions.

FAST RUNNING TAKES MORE OUT THE LEGS

Runners in their 40s and 50s can sometimes do the same workouts they ran in their 20s and 30s—but they will pay dearly for this. Running at your limits, after a certain age, takes an increasingly longer recovery time. While it is true that speed training and racing significantly increase the chance of injury, there are safer ways to train to improve times at any age. As you age, recovery elements must be added to the program (longer rest between speed repetitions, complete rest the day before a speed workout). I don't recommend speed reps after 80 years of age, but there is some speed benefit from my Cadence Drills and Acceleration-Gliders, mentioned in this book.

FINE-TUNING FROM PREVIOUS YEARS

As much as we would like to improve memory, this will probably not happen. Making good notes in your journal will allow you to analyze the causes of aches and pains, and training problems. Even if you can't run faster at age 90, you can run smarter, and prevent problems. Use the margins of your journal. Tell yourself what you want to do the next time, to avoid problems. You'll help yourself greatly by tracking the adjustments. As you embark on another goal in future years, you'll have a better blueprint, because you've improved the original plan through adjustments to your reality.

I believe that a great deal of the satisfaction we receive, emerges from what we do on a regular basis. I've seen many people improve their outlook on life itself when they use a proven plan to improve their fitness. Following and adjusting your plan is almost always a life-changing experience, for the better.

BLOOD SUGAR ISSUES

Many exercisers develop blood sugar problems as they age. Read the chapter in this book on blood sugar maintenance.

HEALTH ISSUES

Running and walking make you feel better as they enhance health potential and life expectancy. Many runners have told me that their running gave them the only signs of serious health risks—which led to early detection and successful treatment. Find a doctor who supports running and wants to work with you to sustain the highest level of wellness.

WHAT DO YOU WANT OUT OF YOUR RUNNING?

This is the most important question for anyone to answer—but especially for runners over 40. For me, the answer is simple—I want to be able to run almost every day, injury-free, for the rest of my life. That is why I slow down and walk often. My ego has been able to adjust to slower running, and I know that I feel better every day because I run slowly.

As I mentioned in the first chapter, you are the captain of your running ship. If you want to run a certain distance every run, or not run slower than a certain pace, or win your age group in the local road races, it is your right to go for it. With these as your goals, be sure to have the phone numbers of your sports medicine doctors handy. But for each goal, you must take responsibility for the consequences. In other words, if you get injured by trying to stay up with a runner or group that is faster than you, realize that you put this on yourself.

You have lots of choices as to what you want to see as your final running product, each day and each year. Think carefully and structure accordingly.

A SERIES OF LITTLE THINGS...

- Making a "social run" into a race. It is too easy to get led astray when we are feeling good. Older runners will often find that their running cadence and stride mechanics can feel easy at the beginning of a run, and sometimes at the end. But the next day, and the day after, it is a different story.

- Trying to run no slower than a certain time is a losing battle—especially on warm days, hilly courses, etc. Mind games work against us as we get older. Your mind can remember when a certain pace was easy and will get you focused to stay on track for that goal. It is better to be flexible with distance, pace, course, and weather.

- Junk miles are short runs on days that would be better spent as non-running recovery days. In almost every case it is better to take the day off on a short mileage day—and add the miles to other running days that week.

- Starting runs too fast—even a few seconds per mile—produces much greater fatigue. Your legs will feel so much better if you run slower than you could run, during the first 2-3 miles of a run.

- Overstretching—tears muscle and tendon fibers and increases healing time for all runners. This damage takes longer to repair as you get older. It doesn't take much of a stretch to be an overstretch. Since I've not found stretching to be of benefit for almost all runners/walkers I've worked with, I don't recommend it. If you like to stretch, be very careful.

- Pushing beyond your speed or endurance limit for a mile or more will greatly increase the time needed for recovery. Even younger runners must pay for these violations. Older runners pay by not having legs that are bouncy and resilient for a significant period after pushing too hard—or by producing an injury.

- Running and walking form violations produce more fatigue and muscle damage as we age:
  - striding too long
  - bouncing too high off the ground (even half an inch too high)
  - kicking behind you too far

  Refusing to take walk breaks (shuffle breaks) more often because it is too "wimpy". I'm proud to be a wimpy runner who runs every day—instead of being forced to be a couch sitter because of never taking a walk break.

Chapter 25

PRODUCTS THAT ENHANCE RUNNING

The following products will help all runners. For more information on these, visit www. JeffGalloway.com.

Other Galloway books: training schedules, and gifts that keep on giving—even to yourself

(Order them, autographed, from www.JeffGalloway.com)

Running Until You're 100. In the chapter on joint health, you'll see in the research studies that runners have healthier joints than sedentary folks. In the chapter on the researched health benefits of exercise, an expert on longevity says that for every hour we exercise we can expect to get back 2 hours of life extension. Among the heroes section is an 85-year-old who recently finished his 700th marathon and plans to run more. There are nutrition suggestions from Nancy Clark, training adjustments by decade, and many other helpful hints for running past the century mark.

Fit Kids—Smarter Kids. This book is a handbook for parents, teachers, youth leaders on how to lead kids into fitness that is fun. A growing number of studies are listed that document how kids who exercise do better in academics, and in life. Nancy Clark gives tips on what to eat, and there's a chapter on childhood obesity—with the hope that others, like the author (a former fat kid) can turn things around. There are resources, successful programs, inspirational stories and much more.

Women's Complete Guide to Running & Women's Complete Guide to Walking. By Barbara and Jeff Galloway. The section on woman-specific issues makes these books unique: pregnancy, menstrual issues, bra-fitting, incontinence, osteoporosis, inner organs shifting, menopause and more. There's a section for the unique problems of the "fabulously full figured" runners. Nutrition, fat-burning, motivation, starting up, aches and pains—all are covered in the book. There's also a section in each book written by famous sports nutritionist Nancy Clark.

Walking. Walkers now have a book that explains the many benefits, how to maximize them, with training programs for 5K, 10K, half and full marathons. There is resource information on fat-burning, nutrition, motivation, and much more.

Running: Getting Started. This is more than a state-of-the-art book for beginners. It gently takes walkers into running, with a 6-month schedule that has been very successful. Also included is information on fat-burning, nutrition, motivation, and body management. This is a great gift for your friends or relatives who can be "infected" positively by running.

Running: A Year Round Plan. You'll find daily workouts for 52 weeks, for three levels of runners: to finish, to maximize potential, and time improvement. It has the long runs, speed sessions, drills, hill sessions, all listed, in the order needed to do a 5K, 10K, Half and Marathon during one year. Resource material is included to help with many running issues.

Galloway's Book on Running. This is the best-seller among running books since 1984. Thoroughly revised and expanded in 2001, you'll find training programs for 5K, 10K, half marathon, with nutrition, fat-burning, walk breaks, motivation, injuries, shoes, and much more. This is a total resource book.

Marathon: You Can Do It! This has the information you need to train for the classic event. There are training programs, with details on walk breaks, long runs, marathon nutrition, mental marathon toughness and much more.

Half Marathon: You Can Do It! This new book provides highly successful and detailed training schedules for various time goals, for this important running goal. Information is provided on nutrition, mental preparation, fluids, race day logistics and checklist, and much more.

Running: Testing Yourself. Training programs for 1 mile, 2 mile, 5K, and 1.5 mile are detailed, along with information on racing-specific information in nutrition, mental toughness, running form. There are also some very accurate prediction tests that allow you to tell what is a realistic goal. This book has been used effectively by those who are stuck in a performance rut at 10K or longer events. By training and racing faster, you can improve running efficiency and your tolerance for waste products, like lactic acid.

RUNNING SCHOOLS AND RETREATS

I conduct motivating running schools and retreats. These feature individualized information, form evaluation, comprehensively covering running, nutrition, and fat-burning.

THE STICK

This massage tool can help the muscles recover quicker. It will often speed up the recovery of muscle injuries or Iliotibial band injuries (on the outside of the upper leg, between knee and hip). This type of device can warm up the leg muscles and reduce the aggravation of sore muscles and tendons. By promoting blood flow during and after a massage, muscle recovery time is reduced.

To use "the stick" on the calf muscle (most important in running), start each stroke at the achilles tendon and roll up the leg toward the knee. Gently roll back to the origin and continue, repeatedly. For the first 5 minutes a gentle rolling motion will bring additional blood flow to the area. As you gradually increase the pressure on the calf during an "up" stroke, you'll usually find some "knots" or sore places in the muscles. Concentrate on these as you roll over them again and again, gradually breaking up the tightness.

FOAM ROLLER—SELF-MASSAGE FOR IT BAND, HIP, ETC.

This cylinder of dense foam is about six inches in diameter and about one foot long. We've not seen any mode of treatment for Iliotibial band injury that has been more effective. For best effect, put the roller on the floor, and lie on your side so that the irritated IT band area is on top of the roller. As your body weight presses down on the roller, roll up and down on the area of the leg you want to treat. Roll gently for 2-3 minutes and then apply more pressure as desired. This is actually a deep tissue massage that you can perform on yourself. For IT band, we recommend rolling it before and after running.

CRYO-CUP—BEST TOOL FOR ICE MASSAGE

Rubbing with a chunk of ice on a sore area (when near the skin) is very powerful therapy. We know of hundreds of cases of achilles tendon problems that have been healed by this method. The Cryo-Cup is a very convenient device for ice massage. The plastic cup has a plastic ring that sits on top of it. Fill it up with water, then freeze. When you have an ache or pain that is close to the skin, take the product out of the freezer, pour warm water over the outside of the cup to release it, and hold onto the plastic handle like a "popcicle". Rub constantly up and down the affected area for about 15 minutes, until the tendon is numb. When finished, fill the cup, and place in the freezer. In my experience, rubbing with a plastic bag of ice—or a frozen gel product—does no good at all in most cases.

ENDUROX EXCEL

Many runners over 50 years old have told us that they have noticed a significantly faster muscle rebound when using this product. An hour before a long or hard workout, I take two of these Excel pills. Among the anti-oxidants is the active ingredient from gensing: ciwega. Research has shown that recovery time is reduced when this product is taken. We also use it when our legs have been more tired than usual for 2-3 days in a row.

ACCELERADE

This sports drink has a patented formula shown to improve recovery. Drinking it before and after prolonged, dehydrating workouts also helps to improve hydration. We recommend having a half gallon container of Accelerade in the refrigerator. Drink 4-8 oz every 1-2 hours, throughout the day. Best time to "top off" your fluid levels is within 24 hours before a long run. Prime time for replacing fluids is during the 24 hour period after a long run. Many runners have 32 oz or so in a thermos, for sipping during walk breaks in a prolonged speed training session. I suggest adding about 25% more water than recommended.

Research has also shown that drinking Accelerade about 30 min before running can get the body's startup fuel (glycogen) activated more effectively, and may conserve the limited supply of this crucial fuel.

ENDUROX R4

This product has almost "cult following" status among runners. In fact, the research shows that the 4:1 ratio of carbohydrate to protein helps to reload the muscle glycogen more quickly (when consumed within 30 min of the finish of a hard or long workout). This means that the muscles feel bouncy and ready to do what you can do, sooner. There are other anti-oxidants in R4 that speed recovery.

JEFF GALLOWAY'S TRAINING JOURNAL

Some type of journal is recommended to organize, and track, your training plan. JEFF GALLOWAY'S TRAINING JOURNAL can be ordered from www.JeffGalloway.com, autographed. It simplifies the process, with places to fill in information for each day. There is also space for recording the unexpected thoughts and experiences that make so many runs come alive again as we read them.

Your journal allows you to take control over the organization of your training components. As you plan ahead and then compare notes afterward, you are empowered to learn from your experience, and make positive changes.

VITAMINS

I believe that most runners need a good vitamin to boost the immune system and resist infection. There is some evidence that getting the proper vitamin mix can also speed recovery. The vitamin line I use is called Cooper Complete. Dr. Kenneth Cooper (founder of the Cooper Clinic and the Aerobics Institute), is behind this product. In the process of compiling the most formidable body of research on exercise and long-term health I've seen anywhere, he found that certain vitamins play important roles.

BUFFERED SALT TABLETS TO REDUCE CRAMPING

If your muscles cramp on long or hard runs, due to salt depletion, this type of product may help greatly. The buffered sodium and potassium tablets get into the system more quickly. Be sure to ask your doctor if this product is OK for you (those with high blood pressure, especially). If you are taking a statin drug for cholesterol, and are cramping, it is doubtful that this will help. Ask your doctor about adjusting the medication before long runs.

CONTROL OVER PACE BY GPS AND OTHER DISTANCE-PACE CALCULATORS AND SMARTPHONE APPS

There are two types of devices for measuring distance, and both are usually very accurate: GPS and accelerometer technology. While some devices are more accurate than others, most will tell you, almost exactly how far you have run/walked. These will allow you to gain control over your pace—from the first 10th of a mile.

Freedom! With these devices, you can run/walk your long ones wherever you wish, instead of having to repeat a loop—just because it is measured. Instead of going to a track to do a "magic mile", you can very quickly measure your segments on roads, trails or residential streets.

The GPS devices track your movements by the use of navigational satellites. In general, the more satellites, the more accurate the measurement. There are "shadows" where the signals cannot be acquired: buildings, forest, or mountains. On trails with lots of small turns, the device may cut the tangents as it accounts for the mileage. These are usually temporary interruptions, but will tend to give a mileage reading that is less that the distance you actually ran/walked.

The accelerometer products require a very easy calibration and have been shown to be very accurate. The two leading brands offering this technology are Polar and Nike. The "chip" on your shoe, is very sensitive to movement and effort, and sends the data to the wrist monitor. I've not heard of any pattern of technical interference with this technology. I've found it best during the calibration, to use a variety of paces, taking a walk/shuffle break or two in order to simulate what you will be doing when you run/walk.

Some devices require batteries, and others can be recharged. Experienced staff members at a technical running store can often advise you on the pros and cons of each product. Sometimes they'll also share the "gossip" on the various brands and models, gained from the feedback they receive from customers.

CREDITS

Cover Illustration:	©AdobeStock
Cover Design:	Anja Elsen
Photos:	©AdobeStock
Interior Design and Layout:	Annika Naas
Managing Editor:	Elizabeth Evans